CONTENTS

FOREWORD

In the world of short-form content—where Ashley and I first connected—it's hard to keep someone's attention. We all live in a scroll-and-swipe world. But when I started reading *The Manager Method,* I didn't want to put it down. It felt conversational and flowed so naturally that it felt like drinking water—refreshing, grounding, and exactly what you didn't realize you needed. Every page just made sense. Ashley doesn't write about management in the abstract; she writes about the real, human situations we've all seen or been through.

What makes her voice so compelling is the way she brings together humanity and practicality. There's no jargon, no corporate spin—just clear, actionable tools grounded in stories that ring true. Reading this doesn't feel like being lectured; it feels like sitting down with a mentor who understands the messiness of leadership and wants to help you navigate it with confidence.

The perspective here is a welcome break from the old "command and control" style so many of us were taught. Ashley shows us that leadership isn't about being flawless or authoritarian—it's about being present, empathetic, and intentional. It's about showing up for your team in ways that build trust, resilience, and results, even in uncertain times.

And throughout the book, there's a reminder that shouldn't be overlooked: Managers matter. They can be the difference between someone dreading Monday morning and someone feeling energized to contribute. In today's unpredictable world of work, that influence has never been more critical—and Ashley equips you with the clarity and confidence to lead in a way that makes a real difference.

My hope is that you find what I did in these pages: practical guidance, stories that feel like your own, and the steady encouragement that you're more ready for leadership than you may think.

— **Steve Cadigan**

LinkedIn's first Chief Human Resources Officer
and author of *Workquake*

PREFACE

When Ashley asked me to write this Preface, I couldn't help but think deeply about the journey that brought us both here. As a mother, nothing makes you prouder than seeing your child create something meaningful—something that not only reflects their values but also inspires others to grow.

My own journey was far from traditional. I graduated college later in life, then law school in my 50s, and beat cancer not once, but twice. Along the way, I grew my career from an intern at a state agency to retiring as general counsel. If there's one thing I've learned, it's that perseverance, a willingness to keep learning, and the ability to lead with empathy can take you further than you ever imagined. These principles were the foundation of my own leadership, and they resonate so very strongly with the lessons Ashley shares in this book.

The Manager Method is more than a guide to being a great manager—it's a call to treat people with respect, empathy, and fairness. I've watched Ashley grow into someone who cares deeply about empowering others to lead, not just with their heads but also with their hearts.

As I reflect on my own career, I see how many of the principles in this book shaped the way I worked and led others. From focusing on clear communication to making thoughtful decisions under pressure, these tips are not just words on a page—they're practical tools that create real impact.

Whether you're an experienced manager or managing a team for the first time, this book is a reminder that leadership is a journey, built one thoughtful decision at a time. Just as I've found strength and success through these approaches, I hope you'll find inspiration in this book to create your own ripple effect of support, positive impact, and meaningful progress.

Ashley, I'm so proud of you, and I can't wait to see the impact this book will have.

With love and admiration,
Mom (aka Nancy Vinsel)

INTRODUCTION

What No One Tells You About Leading People

Being a manager can be like trying to walk four dogs at once—one's chasing a squirrel, another's barking at the mailman, the third is lying down and refusing to move, and the fourth is trying to get you to stop and give them belly rubs—immediately. Does that hit home . . . a little *too* closely?

In other words, have you ever worked with a group of individuals who all bring different personalities, work styles, and perspectives to the table and found yourself thinking, <u>*Why*</u> *is this so complicated?* Maybe you're in the middle of a conversation with a team member and they ask something that leaves you thinking, <u>*Why*</u>* *would they ask that?* Or you review their work, and you can't begin to figure out, <u>*Why*</u> *did they approach it this way?* These moments can make you question whether this whole "manager thing" is really for you. And regardless of what's happening, you're left asking yourself, *What am I actually supposed to <u>do</u> now?*

As a manager, you're not alone in feeling this way. Every leader—whether they're just starting out or have years of experience—struggles with these same questions. It doesn't matter whether you're talking one-on-one with a new team member or sitting in a corporate boardroom as an executive; figuring out *why* your team does what

---

*   It may actually be *"Why the @%!"* but this is a family-friendly book.

they do and *how* best to respond is something every manager has to work through.

Here's the thing: If you're feeling overwhelmed and questioning whether you're cut out to be a manager, know that many people out there feel like they'll never have a manager who truly cares about or supports them. I see it all the time in comments on social media when I post role-play videos of good leadership. People say things like, "This is fiction" or "This doesn't happen in real life." Those comments used to really bother me. It can be hard to hear those time and again and not give up posting videos (or being a manager, if you've heard those, too). But over time, I've realized that these reactions usually come from people who've likely had awful experiences themselves or seen friends and family go through them. It's a defense mechanism to assume that good managers just don't exist. But even for those who've had the most unfair and awful experiences at work (which no one deserves), I believe there's always hope for things to get better and for the chance to work with a manager who truly cares. After all, people aren't expecting perfection from managers, just someone who's honest with them, helps them do well, and makes them feel like they matter.

This is where you come in. With a few simple actions, you can become the manager every employee deserves—the one who not only guides but also supports and inspires. It doesn't matter how much experience you have or whether you wish you had done things differently in the past. What matters is that right now, you can be the leader your team needs.

As you reflect on your career and think about what you can do to be that great manager, first consider the managers and colleagues who've impacted you. That impact may be good . . . or not so good. Were they the ones who made you dread showing up on Monday mornings, or were they the ones you admired and wanted to be like? Often, the most memorable lessons come from seeing examples of what you *don't* want to become. If you've had those kinds of managers, you didn't deserve that treatment. It shouldn't take experiencing poor leadership to drive you to become a better leader—the kind of leader who makes people feel valued, like they matter, and who motivates them to bring their best to work every day.

Every one of us has had people influence us in our professional lives—both positively and negatively. And that influence shapes how we lead today and how we want to make others feel. From first starting my career as a sandwich artist at Subway to working in retail, grocery stores, and even a golf driving range, until I joined corporate, I rarely took time to reflect on what kind of managers I had and how they impacted me. Instead, I went through life venting about the tough bosses and only truly appreciating the great ones long after the fact. But one of the perks of getting older (there are some!) is learning to be intentional. For me, that means reflecting on my experiences with different leaders—how they shaped me and how I can turn those experiences into something positive. Initially, it helped me define the kind of leader I wanted to be as I stepped into management. Now, it drives me to use my voice to advocate for and support managers and their teams.

You might know me from social media, where I started posting videos in 2022 as @managermethod. Many of those videos are roleplays, where I'm an HR leader talking to a fictional "bad boss" named Luke and calling out the small (and sometimes not-so-small) changes he needs to make as a leader. Sometimes the videos are focused on common issues, like not blindsiding employees with negative feedback in performance reviews. Other times, I cover legal topics, like what to consider about women needing to pump at work after maternity leave. I started making those videos as a creative outlet as I was building my manager training business. And I soon heard that those social media videos *were* training. People commented and messaged that they liked my videos and learned from them.

Sometimes people asked what my background was, other than a face on their screen. It's a good question, and if I'm giving you advice in this book, you might be wondering the same thing. Fair enough. Let's talk about it.

MY ROAD TO MANAGER METHOD (WITH SOME STOPS ALONG THE WAY)

I started working at age 15, and before I ever set foot in a corporate office, I held a whole range of jobs—Subway sandwich artist, Kmart electronics associate, Winn-Dixie cashier, server at an Italian restaurant, golf driving range assistant, U.S. census worker, economics research assistant, and HR intern at the Glimmerglass Opera House in Cooperstown, New York. Part of the reason I racked up so many titles is that the first five places shut down not long after I'd worked there.* I won't dwell on these roles, but I will explain shortly how these experiences shaped what I do now.

From there, I began my corporate career in consulting sales, spending two years cold-calling and selling to chief financial officers and heads of human resources before going to law school (I highly recommend cold-calling if you ever want to thicken your skin). I worked as a lawyer, first at a law firm and then in-house, working directly for companies, including in their legal departments, before shifting to HR. That changed my life. As a lawyer, I'd spent years being a situational janitor (a term I've found resonates with many other roles) and cleaning up other people's issues. But in HR, I had the chance to be proactive—to actually help employees succeed in their roles and help managers lead their teams.

I knew from sitting in board meetings and strategy sessions that it's important to meet goals and get business results. It literally keeps the lights on and keeps people employed. But I also saw that how managers treat employees can deeply affect how people feel at work, which impacts their retention (how long they stay) and engagement (how much they care about their work).

You may hear others at work talk in those terms—retention and engagement. I've never been a huge fan of corporate speak. It may be from reading one too many legal memos that seemed to charge (a lot) by the word. I know it can be easy as a manager to use "big words" to sound smart, but I think speaking more like a real person conveys messages far better. So, put simply, I know that how people feel at work matters—it directly impacts what they get done at work

---

* I can thank the economics position for teaching me that "correlation is not causation."

and how they live outside of work. I realized just how true that was during my time as a lawyer.

This shift happened when I moved from being a law firm lawyer to an in-house company lawyer. I was then in my early 30s and had been practicing law for four years. Most career coaches would tell you to never run *from* a job, but run (or at least apply) *to* a job. This means you should look forward to something about the new role instead of just trying to escape your current one. I didn't follow that advice.

I was definitely running from a job—and not a particular job, but the law firm environment. In law firms, this often means billing hours (meaning writing 0.1 every time you get a six-minute phone call and writing in fairly excruciating detail what you talked about so the client will actually pay the bill), working around the clock, and feeling like every lawsuit is a fight with opposing counsel. It left me drained. I also had a toddler and didn't like the person I was for anyone in my life—including myself. I thought about work all the time and barely slept on Sunday nights as I dreaded the week ahead. So, when one of the firm's clients was growing and let me know they were adding a lawyer to their in-house team (and asked whether *I* wanted to be that lawyer), I jumped at the chance. For law firm lawyers, in-house is supposed to be a dream. No more billing hours! No more late hours! I was excited, but also wondering: *Would it actually be like that?* That question was front and center in my mind.

But when I interviewed with the general counsel, did I ask about any of that? Absolutely not. I wanted that job. And I wasn't about to do anything that could hurt my chances. I was afraid that asking about work-life balance would make me look uncommitted.* Especially since the general counsel was a man with a stay-at-home wife and nanny. I wasn't about to mention that my husband and I both worked, how much I loved picking up my daughter from daycare, or that I worried about what would happen if she got sick—or if Atlanta declared it too cold for school to open and I had to stay home. There was no way I was bringing any of that up.

---

* We'll cover this later in the book, so your candidates feel comfortable asking the questions they really want to know about the job.

But during our interview, the general counsel said words that changed my career. He said, "I want to be up front that working in-house comes with a pay cut compared to law firm salaries—that's just part of the trade-off. But one thing you gain is a predictable schedule. You'll work eight to five, with no nights or weekends. We do good work, we have fun, and I think you'll really like the people here." I perked up—hearing my potential future boss bring up working hours (especially what wouldn't be expected after hours), and having fun, was wild. No lawyer talked about that. It was exactly the kind of reassurance I'd been hoping for, but was way too nervous to ask about.

As an epilogue, I got the job, and it lived up to those promises. The predictable schedule and fun working environment were absolutely true. It changed both how I felt about work (I truly looked forward to Monday mornings) and the person I was outside of work, for the better. My friends and family knew how much I loved my job, and it didn't just change my career—it changed my life. That boss remains a mentor and friend to this day.

WHY ONE MOMENT STUCK WITH ME AND WHY IT MATTERS TO YOU

Since then, I've spent a lot of time thinking about why that conversation was so meaningful. You can probably see it already—my boss clearly communicated what the job would be like and followed it up with actions. Simple, right? But it's not as simple in practice. There's so much talk about "setting people up for success at work" *without ever explaining what that means*. But when managers actually understand it—and know how to do it—that's what sets them apart as truly effective leaders. As an employee, my boss telling me, "This is what's expected," and living it out was exactly the recipe that set me up for success. When I was treated like I mattered as a person, I cared more about my work. I showed up to work each day recharged, ready to help and learn from others, confident sharing my ideas—and our "small-but-mighty" team won a coveted award in our industry.

What made my boss decide to create this environment where we did great work but also truly left it behind when we walked out the door each day? Part of the answer goes back to a senior colleague who came long before me. She was honest about wanting to do good work and also be fully present for her family. That took a lot of courage, and I'm grateful that she did that. And it took a lot of humility on the leader's part to be open to—and listen to—ideas from his team, and then implement them. Together, my boss and senior colleague worked intentionally to build systems and templates so we could work within reasonable working hours. It made a difference for all of us who joined the team. And it worked. It made a difference not just for those of us on the team but for our families and friends too, who got a much better version of us than if we'd been run into the ground.

In this book, I'll step into the role of that senior colleague, guiding you on how to become the manager you want to be. I'll show you how to set your teams up for success while also benefiting yourself personally. Each chapter includes questions to help you think through your approach. Being a great manager doesn't mean letting people walk all over you or sacrificing your time and energy for everyone else. Instead, it's about using a method that allows you to regain your time and energy while supporting your team members and helping them grow.

How have I seen this play out in real life? Beyond the thousands of managers I've worked with in my career and now running my own training business, I applied these same techniques when I was a manager myself. Just like the question I used on the first page of this Introduction, I often couldn't understand *why* people at work behaved the way they did. However, I realized that by asking the right questions, I could uncover their motivations and both help them learn and learn from them. My role wasn't to solve every issue for them, but to guide them in making the right decisions moving forward. There's no magic formula for being a great leader, but there are practical steps that can help you become the leader your team needs, no matter where you work.

IS THIS BOOK FOR YOU?

Yes! Because this book isn't just for managers who fit a certain profile. It's for managers in any industry, in any role, in any kind of workplace. I've had those frontline jobs I talked about earlier. And in corporate legal and HR roles, I worked everywhere from Yum! Brands (the parent company of KFC) to the McKinsey & Company consulting firm.

In every role—across industries, from in-person teams to remote workforces, from small businesses to global corporations—I saw the same thing: managers facing the same core challenges. That's what ultimately pushed me to take the leap and start Manager Method in 2019, right after being promoted to the "biggest job" of my career: leading North American HR at McKinsey.

If you know McKinsey, you know. And if you don't—it's arguably the most influential consulting firm out there. I had been a member of the global legal team, working literally around the world (and also around the clock) with many incredible people, but I never really felt like I fit in. For years, I'd dreamed about building something to help managers navigate the tough conversations. Ironically, it was getting that so-called dream job that made me realize . . . it wasn't my dream.

Because after working alongside senior consulting leaders with impressive résumés (and at McKinsey, it felt like everyone but me had at least two Ivy League degrees), I kept thinking about the Subway and KFC managers I knew who could run circles around them when it came to leading people. I saw that an assistant restaurant manager and a senior consulting partner often have more in common than you'd expect. Their challenges? Surprisingly similar. And so are the solutions.

I'm grateful for my "career quilt"—the collection of experiences that have shaped how I work and live. Those experiences pushed me to leave corporate stability behind so I could make a bigger impact, taking the knowledge I'd developed over two decades at some of the world's most respected organizations and turning it into something practical and actionable. They helped me get clear on my North Star.

Because at the end of the day, people want the same things: guidance, support, and someone who believes in them.

WHAT HAPPENS TO MOST MANAGERS—BUT NOT YOU

That's why I started Manager Method—and why I wrote this book. After years in legal and HR roles, I've seen what happens when managers don't have the tools they need. It's not just a business risk—it drains time, energy, morale, and potential from both managers and their teams. It can even drive great people out of management because it feels too overwhelming and exhausting. I'm here to set *you* up for success as you read this book by giving you a clear picture of what's ahead as well as tools to make leading your team feel more doable, less overwhelming, and yes, even fun.

So, how are we going to do that? With real, practical tips you can actually use, whether you're brand-new to management or have been at it for years. Because the truth is, even experienced leaders rarely get the training they need. Too often, people are promoted into leadership roles without real support. They're expected to lead just because they were great at their last job. But being a strong individual contributor and being a great manager are two completely different things.

Leadership is its own skill set—and in many ways, it takes just as much, if not more, intentional learning than the technical skills you started with in your career. That's why I focus on making manager training accessible—whether through social media videos, this book, or full programs—so leaders can get what they need, when they need it, in a way that actually works.

Why is it worth the investment? Because managers make all the difference. When managers are engaged (meaning they care about their work) and help their teams feel the same, it drives incredible results.

When I worked at McKinsey, there was one constant expectation: back everything up with data. And the data here couldn't be clearer. McKinsey's own research shows that the single biggest driver of job satisfaction is an employee's relationship with their manager.[1] It goes beyond work: That same relationship is the second-biggest factor in a person's overall life satisfaction.

That matters, because when people have great managers, it doesn't just impact how they work, it also shapes how they feel. And when people feel supported and valued, it shows up in what they accomplish and how connected they are to their work. And when you zoom out to the organizational level, the ripple effect is undeniable. Gallup's research shows that managers account for 70 percent of what drives employee engagement—and when engagement is high, performance, retention, and results all move in the right direction.

Here are real ways a highly engaged team impacts performance and results:[2]

- 21 to 51 percent less turnover

- 10 percent higher customer ratings

- 23 percent greater profitability

- 18 percent higher productivity

- 28 percent less product shrinkage

- 63 percent fewer safety incidents

- 78 percent less absenteeism

But despite all the data showing how much leadership impacts teams, most managers are never taught *how* to lead. And it's not just new managers—regional leaders, VPs, even executives are often responsible for huge teams and big decisions without ever getting real, practical leadership training.

Wherever you are in your leadership journey—and whatever you think about management—this book is for you. You don't have to feel stuck, frustrated, or burned out. Just like your team, you deserve support too. And while finding helpful guidance isn't always easy, that's exactly what you'll find here. We're in this together—and my goal is to equip you with practical strategies to lead with clarity, empathy, and confidence.

What you'll find here aren't just feel-good theories or abstract concepts. Instead, I'll walk you through a real, actionable method that you can apply to your everyday management challenges. Whether it's connecting with team members from day one, managing different personalities, or delegating responsibilities in a way that benefits both you and your team, these strategies will help you become the kind of leader people remember as their best boss—the one who listened, asked thoughtful questions, and empowered them to succeed. And the results are sure to trickle down.

I've shared some of where I came from and what inspired me to create this book: the bosses who let me work in ways that helped me find *my* version of work-life balance, provided me with opportunities to grow, and offered support when I needed it most. And I'm also (now) grateful for the bosses who served as examples of what I didn't want to become. Each one of them has shaped me in some way—through their leadership styles, their choices, and their impact on my career. They've contributed to the lessons I've learned, both good and bad, and helped me see the kind of leader I want to be—just as your own experiences have likely shaped your path and mindset.

LET'S START WITH *YOU*

As you get into this book, I encourage you to take a few minutes and really reflect on your career so far—who has influenced you, what experiences have shaped you, and the kind of leader you want to become. I shared my background and why I care about this work, but this book is ultimately about *you*. You've got people to lead, choices to make, and challenges to face. Every decision you make helps shape the kind of leader you are—just like the leaders who've shaped you, whether by setting a strong example or by teaching you what not to do. Your leadership path won't always be a straight line. There will be moments of doubt, hard calls, and second-guessing. That's normal.

What matters most is that you're willing to keep learning and growing. The fact that you're choosing to read this book means you're already taking steps in the right direction. You're showing a commitment not only to yourself but also to your team and the people who look to you for guidance. Through the lessons, tools, and strategies in this book, we'll explore what it takes to be the kind of leader who not only gets results but also earns the trust and respect of your team. You're already showing up for them just by being here and investing in your growth as a manager. So let this be the start of your journey toward becoming the leader your team deserves.

You're going to make a lasting impact on your team. And you're here because you want that impact to be a good one—and that speaks volumes. So let's get started.

I mentioned earlier that I have resources designed to go hand in hand with this book, and they're ready for you now at **managermethod.com/book**. These resources start right here with the Introduction and include reflection questions to guide your own thinking, as well as discussion questions you can use for a book club or leadership meeting. Whether you're reading solo or with others, these tools will help you put the ideas in this book into action.

Chapter 1

You've Got This

Why You're More Ready
Than You Think

I recently spoke at my college's leadership forum on the topic of imposter syndrome. In a day filled with inspiring stories of accomplishment, I, ironically, spent my session talking about self-doubt. Before my presentation, a female engineering professor came up to me and introduced herself. She told me she was especially looking forward to my session because when she saw "imposter syndrome" listed on the schedule, the term resonated because she'd felt it since literally the first day of her career. She shared her story about the nerves she experienced when she first became a professor. Natural and common, right? Well, the surprising part was that her anxiety *wasn't* about how her students would react or how well she would teach. Instead, she spent the entire night before her first class obsessing over . . . what to wear.

As she prepared, she realized she'd never had a female engineering professor. This led her to debate back and forth in her mind whether she should dress in a formal suit to appear professional and gain respect or wear something more comfortable and functional because the class was hands-on (and, while it's not the point of the story, in case you're wondering, she chose the suit, believing it would help her be taken more seriously). As she shared the memory with me, she shook her head, reflecting on how much energy she had spent worrying about something that now feels insignificant, but at the time, it completely consumed her thoughts.

She spoke about the relief she felt now, seeing more female engineering professors in the field (adding with a wink that, thankfully, they wear a variety of outfits). She said that, back then, how she appeared to others seemed so important. But as she grew in her career, she realized it wasn't the clothes that mattered. And that truly, her students weren't even really looking at or thinking much about *her*. They were thinking about *themselves* because they were more focused on learning than anything about her personally, including what she was wearing.

I loved the professor's story, and asked her for permission to share it in my talk because it resonated with so many students in the audience who were grappling with similar feelings of self-doubt. Young professionals often assume that as they progress in their careers, they'll magically feel more confident. That happened with this professor. But the reality is often the opposite—sometimes, the more you achieve, the more you question yourself.

What about you? Do you feel more confident now than you did previously in your career? Or do you sometimes (or often) feel more anxious as you've grown in responsibility? This professor's story made me think about how managers, too, often live in fear—fear of failure, fear of not meeting expectations, or fear of being judged for seemingly small decisions. When she recounted her experience, she now laughed at how focused she'd been on something like her outfit. After decades in her career, it seemed silly. Yet, it struck me how relatable this is for so many leaders. Whether it's what you wear, how you handle a meeting, or how you make a decision, these seemingly small concerns often mask the bigger fear: that one mistake could somehow jeopardize your entire career.

Her candor that day echoed something I'd heard many times before and since then: that many managers spend a lot of their time worrying. They worry about how their team perceives them, how they will be remembered by their employees, or how their boss might judge their decisions. Often, managers think that if they're too lenient or approachable, they won't be respected or, worse, their boss might criticize them for being "soft." That worry and fear can lead to decisions driven by panic rather than sound judgment, creating a divide between the manager and their team. When team members see a manager as cold and reactive, they quickly lose trust. But that doesn't have to happen. Because, on the other hand, a supportive manager can have a deeply positive impact—not only on an employee's work but also on their life.

A study from UKG revealed a manager has a greater impact on an employee's health than their doctor or therapist[1]—roughly on par with their spouse or partner. There's a reason that study made headlines—it sounds sensational. A manager? More than a doctor? But when I read that, it made perfect sense. So much of our well-being is tied to our work environment, and our manager shapes nearly all of it. It's not always easy to see the culture of an entire organization, but team culture? That's visible every day, and it's the manager who can define—or impact—it. How a manager interacts with their team, the support they provide, and the way they handle challenges all directly affect the lives of their employees. And yes, I don't just mean *work*. I mean *lives*. Managers worry about how their choices will reflect on their careers, but they also carry the weight of knowing that their decisions affect their team members' lives and, by extension, their families.

Being a manager involves making tough decisions, juggling the expectations of both your team and your boss (and their boss, and so on), and finding a way to do it all sustainably. It can often feel like you're walking a fine line between being too strict and too lenient. I like to call overly strict managers "tight-jeans" leaders. These are the managers who are so focused on making sure their team does everything perfectly that they can end up micromanaging—painfully. This behavior often stems from good intentions—wanting the team to succeed or shielding them from senior leadership's criticism—but it can feel stifling. It's the "toxic behavior" employees often cite in an exit interview, or more commonly, in online employer reviews or conversations with family and friends.

On the other hand, managers who are overly lenient—giving their team too much freedom—are what I call "oversized sweatpants." These leaders might claim they trust their team, but in reality, they're not offering enough guidance or support. They're the ones who say, "My team knows where to find me if they need me!" but would be surprised to learn that their team feels otherwise—because without scheduled meetings, unanswered calls and e-mails pile up, and eventually, people just stop trying. By creating too much space, they leave expectations unclear and fail to inspire motivation or growth. They shy away from giving feedback—even the constructive kind their team needs—because it feels uncomfortable for them. But without direction or honest input, the team ends up feeling lost, uncertain of what's expected, and unclear on how to succeed.

The sweet spot is what I call "cozy joggers" leadership. This is where you strike a balance—you give your team room to breathe, but also provide a clear structure, and you can adjust the structure when needed. You can tighten or loosen the reins based on the situation, but there's always a sense of clarity and flexibility, allowing your team to grow without feeling overwhelmed or lost.

The analogy might sound funny, but I bet it'll come to mind the next time you struggle to squeeze into jeans fresh out of the dryer. And the reality is, this approach doesn't just benefit your team—it helps your career, too. When you genuinely support your team, you don't just earn their respect; you also gain the trust of *your* boss. Because when employees feel supported, they're not only happier and more productive at work, but that well-being extends beyond the office. They become better parents, more engaged partners, and more present friends. Their kids aren't sitting at the top of the stairs, overhearing arguments about "Why do you let them treat you that way?" or "Why won't you stand up to your boss?" Instead of bringing workplace stress to the dinner table, they can actually enjoy their time at home. They know they can come to you with concerns and trust that you'll listen and respond thoughtfully, not with judgment. That's the kind of environment where people flourish, both in their careers and in their personal lives.

As a manager, you may worry, *Am I "tight jeans" leadership or "oversized sweatpants"? Am I getting the job done? Is my boss satisfied with my performance? Am I too lenient with my team? I want to be "cozy joggers"*

. . . how can I do that? These are common concerns and questions (well, especially now for those who have read this book), but they stem from the same fear that makes you feel like you don't belong in your role or that you aren't capable of leading effectively. Let's cut that out and change your mindset completely—and permanently.

My goal with this book is to give you practical strategies to tackle those challenges, strike the right balance between performance and support, and become the leader you've always aspired to be. The story of that professor—who went from agonizing over what to wear to realizing her true value as an educator extended far beyond appearances—mirrors what many managers go through. No matter your leadership style, your personality is what makes you a valuable leader. Whether you're an extrovert or an introvert, a seasoned manager or just starting out, working in a factory, a store, or an office, your perspective matters. There's no single "right" way to lead. The key is learning how to leverage your strengths, make informed decisions, and support your team in a way that benefits both them and you.

If you still worry, *But I can't shake these feelings of self-doubt that creep in,* there are plenty of others—including experts—who agree with you. That's what imposter syndrome is all about. But let's stop those feelings by first stopping calling it "imposter syndrome." Psychologists Pauline Clance and Suzanne Imes coined the term[2] but actually preferred to call it the "imposter phenomenon." They disliked referring to it as a syndrome because it's not a sickness or a disorder; it's something that happens to many people, especially as they advance in their careers. It's that creeping doubt that makes you feel like you don't belong or haven't earned your success— even when you absolutely have. While they first studied it among high-performing women, research has shown that it impacts men as well, and across every profession. The feelings of self-doubt aren't a trend—they're real and extremely common. They can have an impact on careers and lives, from how you feel about work every day to how you actually perform and how long you last in your career.

So, if this "phenomenon" has invaded your thoughts more than you'd like, that's okay. And it's natural. Imposter phenomenon can even grow as you become more accomplished because you wonder whether you truly deserve the responsibility you've been given. You worry about how others see you and whether you're measuring up to the expectations around you.

A big part of managing—and beating—imposter phenomenon is simply acknowledging it and talking about it, which is what this professor did by sharing her story. Many of us struggle in silence, believing we're the only ones feeling this way. The truth is, it's incredibly common, and one of the best ways to overcome it is by discussing it openly. The more you talk about it, the less power it has over you.

That's why, throughout this book, I'm going to ask you to reflect on your own career, your experiences, and those moments of doubt. If you feel comfortable talking about them with your team, colleagues, and friends, it can help them and you. But even if you just want to keep it private for now, *we're* going to talk through what you've learned from your journey so far and how those lessons shape the kind of leader you are today.

YOUR CAREER QUILT

I talked about my career quilt earlier in this book. Take a moment to think about yours. It's made up of all the roles, lessons, and experiences you've had up to this point. Some squares in that quilt may represent challenging times—jobs that were tough or moments when you felt unsure of yourself. Others may represent triumphs, breakthroughs, or periods where you felt confident and found your footing. Each square, whether it represents struggle or success, has contributed to who you are today as a person and a leader. How do you feel when you picture that quilt? Proud? Exhausted? Or do you find yourself cringing at the difficult moments or second-guessing the winding, crooked, "broken" path that brought you here?

Here's the empowering part: You're not broken. Right now, you're a culmination of every step you've uniquely taken, and you have a value like no one else. And no matter where you are in your career, you're growing. You get to choose which squares you focus on as you continue to build your quilt. The experiences you've had aren't just random pieces—they're lessons you can carry forward or set aside, as you see fit. What kind of leader do you want to be? Which squares in your career quilt can help you become that leader? Think about those experiences as you reflect on your career so far, and let that guide you moving forward.

YOUR LEADERSHIP DOUBTS

I always try to meet people where they are. So, take a moment and be honest with yourself—where are you right now? Think about the doubts that creep in. Imposter syndrome often makes us overly focused on how others perceive us. Maybe you worry that being too kind or empathetic will make your team lose respect for you, or that your boss expects you to be stricter. Perhaps you feel insecure because some of your team members have more expertise in certain areas, making you question how to lead them effectively. There might even be moments you look back on with regret, wishing you had handled a situation differently and fearing that others still judge you for it.

Write down some of these doubts. What are the thoughts you keep hidden, afraid that admitting them might make you seem uncertain? Maybe it's that sinking feeling on Sunday nights, wondering whether you're really ready for the week ahead. Or perhaps it's the fear that you're not being firm enough with your team, or sensing that your boss values authority over connection. Whatever it is, acknowledging these thoughts is the first step toward becoming the leader you want to be.

Now, take a moment to step back and remember the same lesson the professor learned—that her students weren't focused on *her*. They were focused on *themselves*. People aren't focused on you nearly as much as you might think. Your team isn't analyzing your every decision or move—they're much more concerned with their own tasks, challenges, and how they can succeed in their roles. They're thinking about how to meet deadlines, improve their skills, or navigate their own work dynamics.

The same applies to your boss. While you may worry your boss is closely monitoring your leadership style or decisions, the truth is, they're probably focused on broader issues—like overall team performance, company goals, or their own responsibilities. Sure, they're paying attention to you. But they're likely more focused on themselves.

The good news is that because people at work aren't analyzing your every move as much as you might think, a few small actions can significantly shape how they perceive you. Focusing on what you can personally do and shifting your mindset away from being overly concerned with what others—whether your team or your boss—think of you can be a freeing experience. Instead of focusing so much on how you're being perceived, direct that energy toward how you can support your team more effectively. Next to the doubts you wrote down, write what your team members are likely focused on and what *they* care about. Then, write what you can do to support them. Focus on helping them achieve their goals, navigate their challenges, and feel confident in their work. You have a mini playbook that can change your mindset and your relationships with your team.

One of the most impactful ways to grow in confidence as a manager is to stop thinking about yourself. This isn't a criticism. It's an invitation. Truly, stop worrying about whether you're being judged and start concentrating on how you can enable your team to succeed. Show up for your team, guide them, and give them the tools they need to thrive. You don't need to be looking around to see whether your team and your boss are looking. They will notice because your leadership will be evident in the success and well-being of the people you're managing.

In fact, this shift in focus away from yourself and toward your team can reduce your own stress and worry, those twin feelings that may have taken up more space in your head than you'd care to admit. Now, instead of wondering whether you're doing enough to prove yourself, you'll feel confident knowing you're helping others succeed, which in turn demonstrates your value as a leader.

TALKING THROUGH IMPOSTER PHENOMENON

But as I've said already, your leadership journey is called a "journey" for a reason. No matter how much you highlight, write notes, and act on the steps in this book, sometimes those old nagging feelings will come back. Talking about those doubts you've written down (and how you'll support your team) can help you conquer them. When we bring our doubts into the light, they lose some of their power. By opening up about these things with other managers and your team, you can support them and encourage them to share their own challenges.

As we go through this book, I'm going to keep meeting you exactly where you are, at the moment you need it. I'll provide practical tools and strategies to help you work through those insecurities, and in doing so, you'll also be giving your team the support they need to succeed. You don't need perfect words or all the answers. Instead, you'll learn how to ask the right questions and guide your team to find solutions.

The goal isn't to eliminate self-doubt entirely—it's to understand that those doubts don't define your ability to lead. It's okay if you don't have everything figured out right now. What matters is that you care about your team and are willing to put in the effort to grow. In other words, it doesn't matter where you begin—what matters is that you're taking steps of self-reflection and action, which is more than many with the "manager" title can say. And you're not doing it alone.

YOUR SUPPORT SYSTEM

Another key to overcoming self-doubt is recognizing your support system. Think about the people in your life who have your back—colleagues, mentors, family, and friends—and write down their names. Who do you turn to for advice when you're feeling uncertain? Who reassures you when you're questioning yourself? These are the people who believe in you, even when you might struggle to see your own strengths. Keep this list handy, and when you're feeling unsure or doubting yourself, don't hesitate to reach out. Sometimes, all it takes is a quick conversation with someone who genuinely believes in you to remind you of just how capable you are.

Reflecting on your support system is a powerful way to stay grounded, especially when imposter phenomenon starts creeping in. It's easy to get caught in a loop of self-doubt, questioning whether you're really cut out for leadership or whether you're making the right choices. But when you remember there are people in your corner who see your potential and value your contributions, it can help shift that mindset. These are the people who will remind you of your past wins, encourage you through tough times, and help you see the strengths you might overlook in yourself.

Even just writing down their names can be a reassuring reminder you're not in this alone. Maybe you have keepsakes from co-workers, notes from family or friends, or even photos you keep nearby as you work. These people care about you. You've got a team of people rooting for you. On those tough days when self-doubt sneaks in, take a deep breath, look at your list, and consider reaching out to one of them. If you feel embarrassed or uncertain doing this, use that same activity and don't think about yourself. Think about them. Most people—especially those who support you—want to be helpful in whatever way they can in the moment. Whether it's a quick text, a phone call, or grabbing a coffee, hearing someone remind you of what you bring to the table can be exactly what you need to keep going. And you'll likely help them too.

Think about the different roles your support system plays in your life. Some people might be great for career advice, while others are more about emotional support or helping you brainstorm ideas. Knowing who to reach out to in different situations can make all the difference. Surrounding yourself with people who lift you up will help you remember that those moments of doubt don't define you. What really matters is your strength, your resilience, and your commitment to growing as a leader.

Wondering whether this actually works? Here's an example from two people who learned it firsthand.

A POWERFUL EXAMPLE: THE STORY OF TWO FRIENDS

At the same leadership conference where I spoke to the engineering professor, during my talk, I highlighted the importance of having a strong support system. To help illustrate the point, I invited two attendees—longtime friends since their own college years—to join me on stage. I asked one of them to share something good about herself—just one thing she felt proud of. She hesitated, visibly uncomfortable, and struggled to come up with an answer.

Not wanting to make her stand on stage with discomfort (especially not at a conference about leadership), I turned to her friend and asked, "What's something you admire about the person standing next to you?" Without missing a beat, her friend rattled off a heartfelt list of her strengths, accomplishments, and amazing qualities. As she spoke, I saw the first woman's eyes fill with tears. Hearing someone else describe her so positively touched her deeply.

It was a powerful moment—a reminder of how hard it can be to see our own worth, even when those around us see it so clearly. I then flipped the exercise, asking the first woman to share what she admired about her friend. This time, the words came easily, and the impact was just as emotional.

The lesson wasn't limited to that stage: Surround yourself with people who uplift you, especially when you're dealing with feelings of doubt. Sometimes, we get so caught up in our own insecurities that we forget all the strengths we hold inside. But hearing someone else acknowledge those qualities can be a powerful reminder of the impact you're already making. That moment at the conference wasn't just touching for those two women—it resonated with everyone in the room, including me. It was a real example of how crucial it is to let others remind us of our value when we can't always see it ourselves. And now you can take the opportunity to see it as well.

ASK SOMEONE WHAT THEY ADMIRE ABOUT YOU

As a final exercise, reach out to someone you trust and ask them to tell you what they admire about you. Yes, I know it might feel a little awkward at first, but it can be incredibly rewarding to hear someone else reflect on your strengths. If you're looking for the right words, try saying something like, "I'm working on recognizing my own strengths, and you're someone whose opinion I really value. Could you share a couple of positive qualities you see in me?" I get it—your stomach might drop the moment you hit send on that text or say it out loud, and you may even second-guess yourself. But trust me, when they share what they see in you, those feelings of hesitation will quickly shift.

When others start pointing out your strengths, it can shift your perspective, helping you see yourself in ways you may never have considered. Often, it inspires you to do the same for them—sharing the qualities you admire, which can make their day and leave a lasting impression they carry with them for a long time. This isn't about creating a forced routine but about recognizing the value of connecting through genuine affirmations when you need a reminder of your worth.

Hearing those positive words helps you step outside the cave of self-criticism and see yourself through someone else's eyes. It reinforces the strengths you bring not only as an individual but also as a leader. And here's the thing: Just like you benefit from hearing words of affirmation, your team does, too.

In this book, we'll explore how to incorporate this into your leadership style—ways to build others up, help your team see their own strengths, and create a culture where recognition and encouragement are a natural part of the day. Taking a few moments to acknowledge the good in others can boost your confidence, theirs, and the overall strength of your team.

Remember, your feelings matter and directly influence your leadership. When you experience confidence and joy, use them as fuel to create even more positive outcomes. When worry and doubt creep in, acknowledge them and take intentional steps to address them. Imposter phenomenon is something nearly everyone faces, especially as you advance in your career. Feeling uncertain is normal, but it doesn't have to stop you. By reflecting on your experiences, talking through your doubts, and leaning on your support system, you can strengthen your confidence and lead with clarity and purpose.

YOU'VE GOT THIS

That's a central theme I want to carry with you throughout this book. You already have the tools to be a great leader—you just need to trust in yourself and continue growing. As we move into the next chapter, we'll dive into what the Manager Method is—a simple, actionable approach that can help you in every situation as a people manager, including navigating the challenging ones you face, to lead with confidence and clarity. Together, we'll work on developing the skills you need to be the leader your team deserves.

Questions for Self-Reflection

(I've included these at the end of each chapter for you to use in the way that feels right to you, whether that's jotting answers in this book, writing in a journal or digital notes, or simply pausing to think. The goal is to take a moment to be intentional and reflect on how the chapter's lessons apply to your own experience and growth.)

- **When have I experienced feelings of self-doubt in my career?**

   Think back on moments when you questioned your abilities and consider how those thoughts might have influenced your actions or decisions.

- **What steps have I taken (or can I take) to overcome those doubts?**

  Reflect on strategies that have helped you build confidence, or explore new approaches that could shift your mindset.

- **How do I think imposter syndrome (or phenomenon) has affected my leadership style?**

  Consider whether your self-doubt has influenced the way you lead your team and how addressing it might change your approach.

- **Who in my life (in or outside of work) has helped me overcome these feelings?**

  Think about the people who have supported you in your journey and how their guidance has helped you challenge those self-doubts. If you haven't reached out to someone, who could you turn to for advice?

- **How can I help my team hear more positive feedback about their work?**

  Reflect on ways you can actively share successes and acknowledge your team members' strengths to boost their confidence and reduce self-doubt.

Chapter 2

The Manager Method

A Simple Formula That Works

During a break in a training session I was leading, a manager approached me and asked if I could give him some advice. He said, "You said we should be honest with our team. But sometimes they ask me something, and I don't really know what the right answer is. I can tell they want help, so I just say what I think I'd do. Then later I might think—*uh-oh, maybe that wasn't right.* And now I don't know what to do. Do I go back and say something? Will they think I don't know what I'm doing? I don't want them to go ask someone else instead, but also, I don't want to mess it up."

None of us wants to mess it up! That conversation stuck with me because so many managers feel the same way, even if they don't say it out loud. When you're the one in charge, people expect you to have the answers—especially when your team's looking right at you, waiting. But the truth is, no one has all the answers. And sometimes, there's more than one "right" way to handle something. Still, most managers don't want to say, "I don't know." It feels like you're failing somehow, like people might not take you seriously if you admit it. But the funny thing is, trying to respond too fast—just to have something to say—can actually cause more problems later on.

I knew exactly what the manager could (and should) have said—and you probably do, too. It all came down to the three simple words he was afraid to utter: "I don't know." Imagine how much easier the situation could have been if he had just said those words, and just a few more.

He could have added, "But what do you think?" to engage the employee in problem-solving. Or he could have directed them to where they could find the answer, collaborated with them to figure it out, or promised to find out and follow up later. That honest and straightforward response could have saved him from the much bigger challenge of fixing everything after the fact.

But I completely understand his hesitation. Even the way he phrased his question to me said it all—he wasn't focused on *finding the right solution*. Instead, he was trying to *avoid doing the wrong thing*. He was operating out of fear, and that's something many of us can relate to. When someone turns to you for guidance, it can be uncomfortable not to feel like you have the perfect answer. As humans, our natural instinct is often to jump in quickly with a solution. But as managers, it's important to recognize that responding under pressure, and out of fear, can often lead to mistakes.

This manager shared that, to him, the real challenge wasn't just giving a wrong answer—it was figuring out how to fix it later in a way that didn't damage his credibility or the trust his team had in him. That might sound familiar. And that's why having a dependable process, to be able to use in every situation as a manager, is so important. A clear framework helps you take a moment to pause, think through your response, and act thoughtfully—building trust and keeping everything on track.

WHEN YOU DON'T KNOW WHAT TO DO

Here's something that might come as a relief: Not knowing what to do immediately is normal. You're human, not a walking encyclopedia. Every workplace is full of complex situations—interpersonal dynamics, competing priorities, unclear expectations, and unexpected problems. And just when you think you've seen it all, something new will pop up to challenge your experience and instincts. Whether you've been managing for four months or forty years, you'll continuously face situations that make you second-guess or reconsider your usual approach. And that's a good thing. It means you're growing.

The real issue arises when managers feel pressured to rush into a decision or provide an answer without fully considering the consequences. That's when small problems can escalate into bigger ones simply because they weren't given the attention or thought they required. In these moments, what you need isn't a perfect answer—it's a reliable approach that helps you assess the situation and respond thoughtfully.

THE MANAGER METHOD: PAUSE-CONSIDER-ACT

This is where Manager Method's three-step process comes in: **Pause-Consider-Act**. It's a simple but powerful framework designed to guide managers through challenging situations where they might not have all the answers. Without a doubt, as a manager, you'll often find yourself in situations you never saw coming. Just when you think you've seen it all, something completely unexpected pops up—it's almost unbelievable, but you can't make it up. And the reality is, you won't always have the perfect solution on the spot.

But that's okay. Leadership isn't about *knowing* everything; it's about navigating uncertainty with confidence and making thoughtful, informed decisions in the moment. This process gives you the tools to do exactly that.

I'll walk through each step of the framework, but below is a guide:

Take a pause, for example. Many managers feel the pressure to respond quickly or decisively, often because they think that's what leadership looks like—fast, confident, and unwavering. But let's take a step back. Think about all the times you've been presented with a new situation at work, whether it's a unique challenge a team member is facing, a conflict that's bubbling up unexpectedly, or a decision that has no clear-cut solution. In these moments, you're not expected to have a perfectly polished answer at your fingertips. What sets great managers apart isn't their ability to react immediately, but their ability to pause and evaluate the situation *before* doing something they wish they'd done differently.

Step 1: Pause

The first (and arguably most crucial) step in the process is **Pause**. When you're facing a decision or question that catches you off guard, your instinct might be to respond right away and provide a solution on the spot. This is especially common in those "fast-paced environments," where the pressure to have an immediate answer is ingrained in the organizational culture. If you're in one of those, it can seem like the culture is to value speed over thoughtfulness, where the person who responds first is valued most. However, this "race-to-response" mentality can be problematic. Rushing to react without enough reflection often leads to poor decisions, miscommunication, and something even worse: new problems that arise because the original issue wasn't fully understood. *Pausing* helps break that cycle, allowing for more thoughtful and effective responses.

Pausing is about taking a breath and giving yourself the time to think. It doesn't mean delaying indefinitely or procrastinating. In other words, *pause* doesn't mean *stop*. It means creating a momentary break between thought and response. It could be as simple as taking a break. Or saying, "That's a great question. Let me think about it for a moment and get back to you." By pausing, you give yourself time to gather more information, consult with others if necessary, or just reflect on the best approach.

In some cases, this pause might last a few seconds as you collect your thoughts. In others, it might mean telling your team you need a day or two (or longer) to consider the best course of action. The key is that you're not reacting purely out of pressure or the need to appear decisive. Instead, you're allowing yourself time and space to make a more thoughtful decision.

Pausing is critical no matter how you're communicating—whether face-to-face, by phone, or online. In face-to-face conversations or phone calls, the pressure to give a substantive answer right away can lead to rushed decisions or miscommunication in the moment. Similarly, with e-mails or chat messages, it's easy to fall into a rapid back-and-forth, especially when the other person expects a quick reply. However, rushing to respond, especially as emotions may escalate, can result in misunderstandings, overlooked details, or decisions that aren't fully thought through. If you have any doubt, just look through a back-and-forth exchange that really reads like . . . an e-mail that should have been a meeting.

Instead of firing off a quick reply, take a moment to really read and think about the message. Ask yourself: *What's the best response here? Do I need to be correct, or is it more important to make or keep the peace?* That pause can make all the difference. It helps you avoid unnecessary back-and-forth and ensures your reply is clear, thoughtful, and actually addresses the issue. By taking a beat before hitting send—just like you would pause in a conversation—you can sidestep misunderstandings and make sure your message lands the way you want it to.

Pausing also has the added benefit of defusing heightened emotions in the moment. If you're caught in a tense conversation or dealing with a challenging situation, pausing allows everyone to calm down and approach the situation with clearer heads. Using reasonable words, especially when you think about how they will be received (some foreshadowing into the next steps in the Manager Method) can often reframe the entire conversation.

Step 2: Consider

The next step is **Consider**, which means taking a moment to view the situation from a different perspective—specifically, through the eyes of the other person. What outcome might they be hoping for? What might they be afraid of? What would you want if you were in their position? This step is about practicing empathy and setting aside personal biases or emotional reactions that could influence your judgment.

As managers, it's easy to unintentionally favor certain team members or let past experiences shape how we view them and their abilities. For example, we might expect too much from a reliable employee because they've always delivered, or unfairly judge another employee based on prior mistakes. These conscious or unconscious biases can affect how we handle each situation. That's why reframing your perspective is so important—it ensures you're responding with fairness and empathy.

Reframing is all about taking a step back and asking yourself, *If I were in this person's shoes, what would I want to happen?* Or even better, think about how you'd want someone you care about—a loved one—to be treated in the same situation. This can be especially helpful when you're feeling emotionally tangled up in the issue.

For me, I think of my grandmother, Gigi. Would I want Gigi rushed into a decision or given incomplete information? Of course not. I'd want her to have the time, support, and clarity to make the best choice possible. Even in the most tense of situations, when I envision Gigi on the other side of it, I soften. This simple exercise reminds me to approach situations with care, and it helps strip away emotional biases that can lead to perceptions of favoritism or unfair assumptions. It's about bringing fairness and thoughtfulness to every decision.

While I like to use a consistent standard when approaching situations (such as thinking about how I'd want Gigi to be treated), it's just as important to adapt your approach based on objective information. Fairness isn't about treating everyone exactly the same—it's about considering each person's unique circumstances.

For instance, a new employee who's still finding their footing might need extra guidance and patience, while a more experienced team member may be able to figure things out on their own and might just need a quick nudge or encouragement. It's also important to remember that even experienced team members may need support during times of change and could feel overlooked if they notice newer employees receiving more attention.

You might read that sentence and think, *I'm a boss, not a babysitter. They don't need their hand held.* But you're not holding their hand. You're considering who they are as a person, and the very real feelings they bring to their work. Taking time to connect with team members can go a long way in showing that you value their contributions, especially for experienced team members you might unconsciously take for granted. Whether it's a quick check-in to acknowledge their expertise or a small gesture of appreciation, giving some recognition—like highlighting their accomplishments in a team meeting or sending a thoughtful note—can reinforce that they're an integral part of the team, not overshadowed by the "bright shiny objects." And you'll learn that bringing that consideration doesn't just make them feel good—it makes them work better.

By using a thoughtful method that combines care with an understanding of individual differences, you create a balanced approach that blends empathy and fairness. Instead of brushing off someone's emotions or jumping to conclusions, you're pausing to consider: *What's the ideal outcome here based on where this team member is right now? Are they overloaded with work? Are they new and still finding their footing? Or are they a seasoned team member who just needs a little extra clarity or some extra recognition?* Taking that moment to reflect makes all the difference.

When you approach each situation with this level of thoughtfulness, you're not just being fair—you're also supporting each person's growth. It helps you avoid the trap of relying on past experiences or assumptions and instead focus on giving team members the guidance they need based on where they are right now. This kind of approach builds trust because your team can see that you're being intentional and considerate, even when everyone is at different points in their development.

Step 3: Act

The final step is **Act,** and it's where everything comes together. Acting is about more than just making a decision; it's about taking deliberate steps to follow through, ensuring that the situation is resolved effectively. There are two critical parts to this step: communication and execution.

First, let's talk about communication. Managers sometimes worry about overcommunicating, thinking they'll overwhelm their team or come across as micromanagers. But in reality, most people wish they had more information. They tend to assume the worst when they don't have it. If an employee asks a question or brings up an issue and doesn't hear back, you may simply have intended to reply but haven't gotten to it yet. However, they might interpret the silence as a sign that you don't care or that their concern wasn't important enough to address. This can lead to frustration, uncertainty, and even a lasting breakdown in trust.

When there are gaps or missing details, people tend to fill them in with worst-case scenarios. Ever gotten an e-mail that just says, *"Call me,"* and immediately felt a wave of panic, only to find out it's about a routine question? Or a vague meeting invite with no explanation, and you instantly think you're getting fired, only to realize it's something minor? When we don't have all the facts, it's natural to jump to negative conclusions.

This happens all the time—at work and in life. When it involves work, the emotions can be even deeper because so much is tied to it, like people's livelihoods and even their sense of identity. When employees don't have certainty—whether it's about their workload, performance expectations, or even their future at the organization—they'll often assume the worst. They'll convince themselves that they're doing a bad job, that you don't like them, or that they're going to get fired—when those might be the opposite of the truth.

That's why being up front and clear from the beginning (or the second-best option, which is *now*) about the realities of the job and its expectations is so important. For example, if there's a busy season where long hours are expected, let your team know ahead of time—and explain how you'll support them through it. And it's important to recognize the distinction between the challenging aspects of a job and the ones that are truly unmanageable. There will always be tough parts of any job, but if things are so difficult they're pushing good people away, it's worth rethinking those aspects where possible. For the parts of the job that can't change, being honest and transparent goes a long way. It builds trust, which helps keep your team engaged, lowers their stress, and allows them to focus on doing their best work instead of worrying about the unknown.

And acting doesn't always mean "doing." Even if you're still figuring things out, it's essential to communicate your progress. Let the employee know you're working on it and explain what steps you're taking. For example, you might say, "I've reached out to [so-and-so] for more information," or "I'm still reviewing the data, and I'll have an update by the end of the day." This not only keeps them in the loop but also reassures them that their concern or question is being handled thoughtfully. By managing their expectations through consistent communication, you prevent miscommunication and maintain their confidence in your leadership.

The second part of act is execution—taking action. Once you've communicated your plan, it's time to follow through on what you said you would do. Acting could mean resolving the issue directly yourself, collaborating with the employee to find a solution, or directing them to someone else who has the necessary expertise. Regardless of the approach, the key is that some form of action needs to be taken. If you don't know the answer to a question, you could find the right resource, ask for help, or work with the employee to figure it out. By taking this action—whether it's big or small—you demonstrate to your team that you're reliable and committed to resolving issues, even if you don't have all the answers right away.

But there's another often-overlooked aspect of acting: following up. Even if you delegate the task to someone else or involve another department, it's important to follow up with the original individual who asked or raised the issue. Far too often, people bring something to their manager's attention and then never hear anything back, leaving them to wonder whether the matter was resolved or just dropped. Following up with that employee ensures they know what action was taken, who handled it, and what the outcome was. It could be as simple as saying, "I spoke with IT, and they've fixed the issue," or "I've connected with HR, and they're going to get back to you directly with the next steps."

This kind of closing the loop is vital because it keeps the lines of communication open and demonstrates accountability. Even if *someone else* acts, you can still make sure the employee knows what's going on. That makes them feel informed and valued. When people see that you're not just passing the buck or dismissing their concerns, but staying involved and ensuring things get resolved, it builds their trust in you as a leader.

When you consistently follow through and follow up, you show your team that you genuinely care about their concerns and are committed to addressing them. This builds trust and reinforces the message that, even if you don't have all the answers right away, you're dedicated to finding solutions and keeping them in the loop. In the end, the act step isn't just about fixing a problem—it's about maintaining trust, transparency, and open communication so that they become second nature.

PUTTING IT ALL TOGETHER

The **Pause-Consider-Act** framework is more than just giving you a way to handle questions or requests from your team. It's about building a habit that can help you manage any situation thoughtfully and confidently. The manager who spoke to me during the break in training wasn't looking for a perfect answer—he wanted a strategy to manage the ongoing demands and questions of his role without feeling like he was just making it up as he went.

This method gives you that. It doesn't mean you'll have all the answers instantly, but it means you'll know what steps you can take next, even if the first step is saying, "I don't know, but let's figure it out." It gives you a consistent approach to rely on, no matter the situation.

Because, as a manager, you're going to work with all kinds of people—different personalities, work styles, and backgrounds. And you'll have to work with each of them to figure out very different situations. While you won't have the answer to every question, you can always **Pause, Consider** the situation thoughtfully, and then **Act** with intention and confidence. Over time, this process will help you grow into the leader your team needs, all while staying composed and confident.

Questions for Self-Reflection

- **How do I handle situations where I don't have all the answers right away?**

  Reflect on moments when you've felt pressured to give an immediate answer and think about how you can embrace pausing before responding.

- **Do I make time to consider each team member's perspective before acting?**

  Think about whether you're factoring in the unique needs, challenges, or circumstances of each individual on your team.

- **How do I communicate with my team after I've made a decision?**

  Consider how you ensure that you're as transparent as possible, keeping your team informed throughout the process, even if you don't have all the answers yet.

- **When was a time I rushed to make a decision and regretted it later?**

  Identify a situation where pausing could have changed the outcome and think about how the **Pause-Consider-Act** framework could help in the future.

- **How do I pause to make sure I'm being intentional about positive feedback?**

  Reflect on whether you actively share and communicate positive observations and how that can boost morale, productivity, and trust.

Chapter 3

Why Keeping Your Team Top of Mind Matters

On a call to prepare for a different training session,* the HR team and I were finalizing the presentation, which we'd titled "Empathy in Action." The goal was to help managers understand how they could apply empathy in different situations, bringing a more human touch to their leadership. The HR team loved the content—they could really see how it would benefit the managers and, in turn, the employees. But they did have one edit.

"Can we change the name of the presentation?" they asked.

I was somewhat surprised, because they were the ones who requested that the session be called "Empathy in Action" in the first place. "Of course," I said (this is often a helpful phrase when an organization has hired you). "But I'm curious—why?"

The response made me realize something I hadn't fully considered before. Although they had originally come up with the session title, this team member made a very valid point: Many managers in the organization might not respond positively to the word *empathy*. While they readily acknowledged it *shouldn't* be this way, they explained (and I agreed) that the term might come across as

---

*   You'll notice a lot of these examples come from working with teams getting ready for and leading training sessions. It's always great to get out of my office (unless they're virtual, which is also fun!) and confirm how much a health care organization has in common with a construction tech company—as well as a government branch, mission-based nonprofit, and even a coffee company.

"soft" to some managers. They were especially concerned about the managers who needed the training the most—those who tended to push their teams (sometimes too hard). Their worry was that the title of the session might unintentionally drive away those managers from attending.

For this team (and many others), it was a valid concern. *Empathy* wasn't a word many managers were comfortable using—or hearing. They might even associate it with a sign of poor work ethic—the opposite of what we were going for. If HR announced, "We're bringing in an external trainer on empathy," some might immediately decline, grumbling, "Empathy? Give me a break. The problem is that nobody wants to work anymore." That was a very real possibility, and I'm glad this team member spoke up. We realized that one of empathy's fundamental lessons—that words matter—wasn't just something *managers* needed to learn. It was something *we* had to apply ourselves when planning the training.

This stuck with me. It got me thinking about the disconnect between where we hope managers are in their understanding of key leadership concepts, like empathy, and where they actually are. Acknowledging that gap is crucial. We (and I) can't assume managers will naturally have a strong understanding of things like "emotional intelligence" or "psychological safety"—or even think positively about those terms—especially if their own managers and workplaces haven't emphasized them before. Using terms like that could easily backfire. This interaction was a powerful reminder for me—and the HR team—that to truly connect with managers and help them grow, we need to start from where they are, not where we wish they were.

WHY EMPATHY ISN'T JUST "NICE"— IT MAKES WORK MORE EFFECTIVE

If you're reading this and thinking, *Okay, but a manager's role is to get work done; I'm not exactly looking to sit around in a circle singing "Kumbaya" either,* you're not alone. I've heard—or sensed—that same feeling from many managers over the years. And I get it (also,

I won't make you sing anything in this book). You may have spent your career in workplaces where emotions weren't part of the conversation, and the focus was solely on results. Maybe empathy feels like a nice idea in theory, but not something that fits into the daily realities of meeting deadlines, hitting targets, and keeping everything on track.

But here's the thing: Empathy isn't about slowing down work. It's not about letting things slide just to be nice. It's about understanding that *how* work gets done matters just as much as *what* gets done. And when you focus on *how,* the *what* naturally improves. Pausing to consider how to act with empathy can have work get done more efficiently—in other words, faster.

This ties back to the story I shared earlier about the engineering professor who was so concerned with how she would be perceived early in her career. She worried about what she wore, how she presented herself, and what leadership was supposed to look like. But as she grew in her role, she realized that there's no one exact blueprint for being a good leader. She didn't have to conform to a specific image—she could lead in her own way.

In the same way, there's no one-size-fits-all for how empathy should show up in *your* leadership. You don't need to change who you are as a manager or use fancy words. What matters is recognizing the importance of meeting your team where they are, understanding what matters to them and how they work best—so they get the results you're expecting—and figuring out how to show empathy in a way that feels natural to you.

Using Pause-Consider-Act in Empathy

The **Pause-Consider-Act** framework incorporates empathy in a practical way, without relying on overly soft or fluffy language. It helps you slow down and think through how you're leading. The first step, **Pause**, is exactly that—take a moment to genuinely think about your team, as people. Step away from the common "work is work" mindset and intentionally focus on them as individuals who have real feelings and motivations.

The second step, **Consider**, is about diving a little deeper. What does each person want in life, including at work? What would you or someone you care about want in their position? Often, it's simple— to feel valued as a human being. So, take the time to consider them. Who makes up your team, and what do you know about them? Are there seasoned employees with years of valuable knowledge? Are there new hires still trying to find their footing? Are they dealing with a tough situation outside of work while doing their best to keep it from affecting their performance? What about the high performers who rarely ask for help or the quieter individuals who might be overlooked? Reflect on how their unique experiences could be influencing their performance and engagement.

As you think about your team members as individuals, that's where empathy really comes into play. It's not about checking the box. It's about understanding that how your team feels—whether they feel supported, heard, or valued—directly impacts how they show up at work. How they approach their tasks, how they interact with everyone they work with and for (whether colleagues, customers, patients, vendors, or others), and ultimately, how much they care about the work they're doing.

This brings us to the final step: **Act**. This is where you put into practice what you've reflected on during the pause and what you've learned through considering your team. Acting with empathy doesn't mean becoming a therapist or solving all of your team's personal challenges—that's not the goal. Instead, it's about acknowledging that people bring their whole selves to work, and how you choose to respond to that reality can have a meaningful impact on both their well-being and their performance. It affects not just their work, but their lives, too.

For example, let's say you have a team member who's not performing like you expect. Maybe they're missing deadlines or their attitude seems off. It's easy to get frustrated, label them as a problem, and start thinking about how you're going to get them out of the organization (maybe you think that's—ideally—by getting them to quit or, if not, telling HR, "It's time to make a change"). But before you react, pause. Consider what might be driving their behavior and what you know—or don't know—about their situation.

Have they mentioned feeling overwhelmed by their workload? Could they be dealing with personal challenges that are impacting their focus at work? What steps could you take to help them— *really* help them? These questions matter because, without asking them, you risk making unfounded assumptions. That can lead to miscommunication, missed opportunities to provide support, and even greater disengagement from your team. And one lesson many managers learn too late is that this approach isn't good for them—or for you.

Acting can mean starting by having a conversation with them that goes beyond pointing out performance issues and telling them to do better. Ask them questions—and not just laying down the law and adding, "Do you understand?" Ask how they're doing, what their perspective is, and how you can support them. Sometimes, simply showing that you care can be enough to help them get back on track.

THE IMPORTANCE OF EMPATHY WITHOUT BURNOUT

One final consideration, especially in the **Consider** phase, is the importance of empathy. As managers, it's critical to understand the challenges, frustrations, and emotions your team is dealing with on a daily basis. However, there's a delicate balance between being empathetic and absorbing too much of your team's stress. Empathy doesn't mean you have to feel exactly what your employees feel or take on their burdens as if they were your own. Instead, empathy is about acknowledging their emotions, understanding their perspectives, and offering support in a way that helps them feel heard and valued—without compromising your own well-being.

This distinction is crucial because, as a leader, you have the potential to become a sponge for your team's stress and concerns. If you absorb too much, it can lead to emotional exhaustion and burnout, making it harder to lead effectively over time. Research from the University of Buffalo underscores this point,[1] showing that leaders who take on too much emotional burden from their teams are at higher risk of burnout. When a manager consistently internalizes the stress of their team members, it can erode their energy, impact decision-making, and ultimately affect their ability to lead with clarity.

That's why it's essential to practice healthy empathy. This involves being there for your team, acknowledging their struggles, and showing compassion—but also protecting your emotional and mental health. Some may call these habits "boundaries," but that word can sometimes carry a negative "me vs. them" connotation, which isn't the intention of creating a healthy balance.

Think of it like being a support beam. You want to be there to provide stability and guidance, but you can't let the weight of others' challenges overwhelm you. As you think about what an employee may be experiencing, consider how you can provide meaningful support while also taking care of yourself. Remember, the rest of your team relies on you, and you can't give your best to others if you're running on empty. It could be something as simple as offering additional resources, providing whatever flexibility you reasonably can, or giving them space to vent. Whatever the case, it's important to help without carrying the full weight of their challenges yourself, because you're not just looking to build good rapport in the moment, but a sustainable career.

This book isn't just for you to highlight a sentence and think, *That would be great someday.* It's about putting things into action now. So, what could you say? If someone on your team comes to you feeling overwhelmed, you might say, "I get that this feels like a lot. Let's figure out what's most urgent and see what support or adjustments could make it easier." It's a way to show empathy while focusing on solutions. Use this as a starting point and shape it into something that feels natural for you—you'll find what works best.

By using your own voice, and how you uniquely apply the **Pause-Consider-Act** framework, you're not just benefiting your team; you're also creating a sustainable pattern to follow in your own leadership. You're showing empathy in a way that builds trust and connection, and you're also creating habits that allow you to be effective without burning out. It's about leading with compassion but also maintaining the energy and focus you need to continue guiding your team in the long run.

In the following chapters, we'll explore how this framework can be applied to specific challenges as a manager, whether it's delivering feedback, managing conflict, driving performance, or supporting team morale. Each scenario will show you how to integrate **Pause-Consider-Act** into your daily interactions, creating a foundation for thoughtful, balanced leadership. It all starts with the ability to pause, take time to think, and then proceed with purpose. With this process in hand, you'll have a toolkit to navigate complex situations with confidence while safeguarding both your team's well-being and your own.

Rethinking Your Team Members: More Than Just "Workers"

Every manager can use reminders that your team members are human beings, not just "workers." Taking the time to consider their challenges, perspectives, and needs doesn't just impact their work—it impacts their lives. And here's the thing: Even if your primary concern is results (like the managers attending the formerly titled "Empathy in Action" training session), this approach still works in your favor. When people feel seen, valued, and supported, they're more engaged, productive, and collaborative with others. Building that connection creates a ripple effect that benefits both your team and your goals.

Showing empathy to your team members doesn't have to be a big, dramatic gesture. It could be something as simple as asking about their weekend or asking about something they've previously shared with you. What can that look like? Imagine you know one of your team members has a child who recently started school. A simple, empathetic gesture could be starting a conversation with, "Hey, how's your little one settling into school? Must be a big adjustment for both of you."

This shows you're paying attention, you care about their life outside of work, and it creates an opportunity for connection. The key is to approach it in a way that feels authentic to you and resonates with your team. These small, thoughtful interactions build trust, and trust is the foundation of a productive, engaged team. It all starts with meeting people where they really are.

And, speaking of that, what happened to the manager training session? We ultimately changed the title of the presentation from "Empathy in Action" to "How to Work Best with the Different Personalities on Your Teams."* Sure, it was a longer title, but it struck a chord with the managers the team most wanted to reach. Those hard-charging leaders showed up because it spoke directly to their concerns and the kind of help they were looking for.

After the session, I conducted a scientific (okay, informal) poll, asking the managers if they would have been less likely to attend with the original title. The HR team's instincts were spot-on. Many of the managers admitted they probably would have skipped the session. But because we reframed it in the way they actually spoke, the same concepts felt relevant, useful, and worth their time—and that made all the difference.

What does it mean to meet people where they are? It's about being flexible—willing to communicate and work in different ways to make adjustments that help get the work done more effectively. When our planning team recognized that the word *empathy* wouldn't resonate, we found another way to frame it. You can do the same. Talk about motivation, engagement, or getting the most out of your people. It's not about the exact words—it's about the understanding that how people are treated impacts their performance and results. It's choosing to be realistic about what people are interested in and ready for, and adjusting your approach accordingly.

It's not just about what to call a training session or meeting. When managing your team, it's important to meet your team members where they are by understanding *how* they think and approach their work. Just as managers best respond to messages framed in ways that resonate with them, team members do the same when their unique preferences and tendencies are asked and considered. Everyone processes information differently—some people excel with clear, detailed instructions, while others prefer the freedom to figure things out on their own. As a manager, recognizing and adapting to these differences allows you to tailor your leadership style in ways that help each team member succeed.

---

* And instead of saying things like "emotional intelligence" and "psychological safety," I substituted more real-talk phrases, like "being aware and considerate" and "not making people afraid to speak up." I still use those today—they cut through the noise and actually stick, way more than the formal terms ever did.

Equally important is reflecting on the training—or lack of it—that your employees have received. Remember that question that I said is so common for managers when an employee makes a mistake or falls short of expectations: "*Why* would someone do this?" The reality is, many employees haven't been properly trained or equipped to succeed. Without that, they're left to wing it and navigate their roles on their own, which often leads to errors or inconsistent performance. As a manager, you'll best lead when you pause and ask yourself whether they've been given the tools and guidance they need. Have they been shown how to do the job, or were they simply thrown into the role and expected to figure it out? When employees lack the right foundation, their performance will inevitably reflect that. By addressing gaps in training and support, even those you would have expected to be filled long before, you can help your team members perform at *their* best.

That doesn't happen on its own. You have to be intentional about filling in those gaps. Once you pause, and then consider how your team has been trained and how they approach their work, you can take actionable steps to fill in any knowledge gaps. Hold regular check-ins where you explain that your goal is to support their growth and ask, "What do you need to feel more confident in your role?" or "Are there areas where additional training might help, like shadowing a colleague, working alongside a peer to learn new skills, or partnering with me as your manager to develop specific approaches for your role?" It's important to explain *why* you're asking the questions, because otherwise, team members assume the worst. And it's important to consider their perspective. Often, team members might feel more comfortable learning from others before having a colleague—and especially a manager—observe them in action.

You can take a phased approach to the training they need, starting with simply asking questions. By proactively initiating these conversations and explaining the purpose behind them, you empower your team members to grow while also addressing potential issues before they escalate. Offering support and training isn't about micromanaging or babying your team—it's about equipping your team with the tools they need to succeed. In the long run, this approach benefits everyone, creating a stronger and more effective team.

PAUSE-CONSIDER-ACT FOR YOUR TEAM MEMBER

Let's give it a try. First, **Pause** and think about someone on your team who isn't performing at their best. Now, **Consider**:

- What might be going on with them?
- Are they facing challenges you're unaware of?
- What motivates them?
- Have you seen them excel in some areas but struggle in others?
- Have they received the support or training they need?
- What steps can you take to better understand their situation and help them succeed?

Then, **Act**.

Sit down and have an open, genuine conversation with them—not just about their performance, but about their experience. Start by framing the conversation in a supportive way to explain why you're asking these questions. You could say something like, "I want to make sure you feel equipped and supported to do your best work. I'd like to hear how things are going for you and where I can help." This helps set the tone and shows that your goal is to help, not to criticize (or, as they may legitimately be afraid, to fire them on the spot).

From there, ask thoughtful questions like, "How are you feeling about your work lately?" or "What's been working well for you, and what feels like a challenge right now?" You might also ask, "What's one thing that you'd like help with?" or "Is there anything making your work harder that we could tackle together?"

By explaining your intentions up front, you make it clear that the purpose of the conversation is to understand and support them, not to point fingers. This approach helps build trust and creates a more collaborative relationship. Even when you're feeling frustrated or stretched thin, taking the time to ask questions and listen can help you learn what's really going on and open the door to solutions.

Sometimes, simply listening and showing genuine care is enough to get them back on track.

Empathy isn't about accepting poor performance—it's about enabling strong performance. It's about understanding that people perform better when they feel valued. Whether you call it empathy, engagement, or just good management, the outcome is the same— you'll get better results, build stronger relationships with your team, and create a more positive work environment.

As you go through this book, you'll see how the **Pause-Consider-Act** framework can be applied in all sorts of situations. It's about finding what works for you as a leader and using it to meet your team where they are, whether they're on the shop floor, at a desk, in the field, or anywhere else their work takes them. You don't need to change who you are, but it's important to consider how you can show up for your team in ways that support them and help achieve results together.

Questions for Self-Reflection

- **How well do I understand the different ways my team members think and approach their work?**

  Take a moment to reflect on whether you've adapted your leadership style to meet each individual's needs and strengths.

- **Has my team received the necessary training and resources to succeed?**

  Consider whether any performance issues may stem from a lack of guidance or training rather than a lack of effort or ability, and how your strong performers could help teach others.

- **Do I make time to listen and understand what's going on with my team members, personally and professionally?**

  Think about how often you pause to check in on your team's well-being, both inside and outside of work, and how that might impact their performance.

- **How do I currently respond to team members who are struggling, and what could I do differently to offer better support?**

  Reflect on whether you've approached these situations with empathy and whether there's room to provide more effective support without taking on all their stress yourself.

- **Do my team members worry more about not getting in trouble with me than about getting it right, or do they focus on meeting my personal preferences instead of doing what they think is best?**

  Reflect on whether your team feels pressure to cater to your personal preferences rather than focusing on the best way to achieve goals. Are they more concerned about avoiding mistakes in your eyes, or about doing what's truly best for the team and the organization?

Chapter 4

Hiring and Onboarding

Bringing in the Right People, the Right Way

A good friend of mine had an experience that highlights why using the **Pause-Consider-Act** framework is so important, especially when it comes to hiring a new team member. She was in a role she loved, with great work-life balance, and talked about how much she liked what she did. I was shocked when we went out to dinner and she told me she was interviewing elsewhere. She said that while she was happy in her role, there wasn't much room for growth. She worried that by not considering other opportunities, she'd miss out. So, when a recruiter approached her about a position at a well-known company that had a good reputation, she decided to go for it, at least to interview. The new role offered significant growth potential, along with the possibility of a substantial pay increase. Taking the mindset of "it can't hurt to apply," she decided to apply for the role.

During the interview process, she was fully transparent. She explained why she was interested—that the responsibilities and growth opportunities appealed to her. But also important to her was maintaining the work-life balance she already had. She talked about how much that balance meant to her and her family, and she made it clear she was looking for a role where she could grow, but in a way that was sustainable, not something that would suddenly uproot her family's schedule. She assumed this transparency might take her out of the running. Instead, the team reassured her, explaining that the role was, in fact, a newly created one, to redistribute workload and improve work-life balance for everyone. Relieved and excited, when she received an offer, she didn't hesitate to accept it. She was excited to have found her "dream job."

Until her first week of work.

During her onboarding, she had introductory calls with employees on different teams. On one, a colleague said, "Oh! So you're the new Kevin."

Confused, she responded, "Who's Kevin?"

The colleague was surprised at the question and explained that Kevin was the last person in her role, but he'd quit because of stress. My friend was in shock (which I knew because she texted me immediately). She had been told it was a new position, not a replacement—and certainly not a replacement for someone who'd burned out. She thought it must be a mistake. But when she asked another member of her team, they sheepishly admitted that it was true. Her predecessor (aka Kevin) did in fact leave because of the workload, but the team member said they didn't want to mention it to protect his privacy. So instead, they decided to tell candidates that it was a newly created role, even though that wasn't true.*

This lack of honesty left a bad taste in her mouth and completely derailed her experience with the company. She (understandably) felt deceived. She was more angry and worried about what stress was to come than being engaged in onboarding, and it wasn't surprising when she decided to leave shortly after. Sadly, this isn't an isolated incident. When managers focus on selling only the highlights of a role just to fill the seat, instead of setting clear and realistic expectations, they set themselves—and the new hire—up for frustration. The result? New employees feel let down by a job they were once excited to get, and managers end up right back where they started: reopening the role and restarting the hiring process.

---

* If you're wondering, *What should you say instead in this situation?*, I'll talk about that in just a few pages.

BEFORE YOU HIRE: BE REAL AND
SET PEOPLE UP FOR SUCCESS

What's your response to reading this story? Are you most surprised that a candidate would bring up work-life balance during the interview process? For some, it might seem bold or even inappropriate to discuss personal priorities so openly, especially when you feel the need to prove yourself to even earn the job. But in reality, being transparent about what matters—when done thoughtfully—can demonstrate strategic thinking. It shows the candidate isn't just focused on securing an offer or announcing a new role on LinkedIn; they're genuinely invested in understanding what the position entails and ensuring it's a sustainable fit for the long term.

This story points to a problem a lot of organizations run into: making a role sound amazing without giving a real picture of what the job is actually like. As a manager, it's easy to focus on the positives to make a great impression and get the best candidate. And, of course, candidates often do the same, playing up their strengths and glossing over their gaps to "win" the job. Interviews can start to feel like a reality competition, instead of a real conversation to figure out whether it's a good match. But if you're not up front about what the role really involves, it can lead to frustration and disengagement—for the new hire, the team, and even you as the manager when that "dream candidate" leaves sooner than expected. Sure, it can feel uncomfortable to slow down and have honest conversations, especially when you're in a rush to fill the opening. But taking the time to set clear expectations up front is the key to making sure everyone's set up for long-term success. To do that, before jumping immediately into hiring, **Pause** to **Consider** the critical question: Why is this role open?

While sometimes it's a new position, more often it's replacing someone who left. There can be plenty of reasons people leave— from their own personal needs, to aspects of the current role, to their own career goals. It's tempting to chalk that up to a "bad fit" and start a search from scratch—but repeating the same approach without reflection can lead to the same outcome. If multiple people have left or struggled in the role, that's a signal to reexamine the job structure before filling it again.

Being honest—both with yourself and with candidates—can build trust and set up the next hire for success. If you've already made improvements, say so. If not, acknowledge the challenges and share your plan to support the new hire. And if the job hasn't changed despite past concerns, you'll need to be realistic about the expectations and prepare to support the person stepping in as best you can.

To make a strong case internally, especially if you're facing resistance, tie your feedback to costs. Leaders are more likely to act when they see the business impact. Research from *Harvard Business Review*[1] and Gallup[2] shows the cost of replacing an employee can range from 50 percent to over 200 percent of their annual salary, depending on the role. That includes recruiting, onboarding, and lost productivity. By tracking turnover data and linking it to exit interviews or survey feedback (like stress, poor support, or unclear expectations), you can make a better case for changes that improve retention and performance.

You don't always have to be the bearer of bad news and talk about worst-case scenarios. You can frame the conversation around what's possible, like how sustainable workloads actually drive better long-term results. Even if the team is hitting their goals now, a more balanced setup can lead to even stronger performance. And when employees feel supported and the expectations are realistic, they're more likely to stick around, stay motivated, and do better work. And that's not just a nice-to-have—it's been shown to boost overall organizational performance, including higher profitability and, when it applies, even stronger stock prices.[3] (That part usually gets leadership's attention.) Before we walk through how the **Pause-Consider-Act** formula can help guide these decisions, here are a few key tips for hiring and onboarding that can make a real difference from day one.

HIRING TIPS: START WITH DAY ONE IN MIND

Once you've reflected on why the role is open, the next step is getting clear on what success looks like—not just in the job description, but in real life. Before you post the opening or start interviews, take a few minutes to define what you actually *need* on day one. What does a candidate absolutely *have* to know, or be able to do? What can be trained over time? What would make someone successful in their first 30, 60, or 90 days? Focus on what the role really requires now and what support they'll need to grow into more. That balance of clarity, honesty, and support is what builds strong hires—and strong teams.

Then, structure your hiring process around that, all designed to find the best* candidate. If strong collaboration is critical, include it in your interview questions. If success depends on being able to manage competing priorities, give them a scenario to work through. The more aligned your process is to the actual work and team dynamic, the better your chances of finding someone who's set up to succeed—and stay.

FROM OFFER TO ONBOARDING: WHAT YOU CAN DO AS A MANAGER

When you finally fill a role, it's such a relief. You've found the right person, they've accepted the offer, and you're thrilled they're starting soon. It feels like a big win—until their first day sneaks up on you, and suddenly, you realize that you haven't done anything to prepare because you don't have any time. Sound familiar?

Consider it from the new hire's perspective: They show up excited but also nervous (but trying not to show that). But when they arrive, things aren't quite ready. Their desk or workspace isn't set up, their equipment hasn't arrived, people on the team don't know who they are, and there's no clear plan for their first day, let alone the days and weeks after that. That awkward first day? It's not exactly the warm welcome they were hoping for, and it can leave them feeling a little deflated and immediately questioning whether they made the right decision.

---

* I intentionally say the "best" and not the "perfect" candidate, because perfect candidates rarely exist. And if you wait too long expecting Mary Poppins to arrive from the sky, you'll likely miss a lot of strong, capable people who—with the right support—could be exactly what your team needs.

Now, imagine the flip side. Your new hire arrives, and you're prepared. Their workspace is ready, or they got a care package with equipment and some goodies, they're greeted warmly, and the team is excited to meet them. You've got a clear onboarding plan in place, so they know what to expect and can start to ease into their role, replacing the nervousness with confidence. They feel valued and supported, which helps them hit the ground running. It sets the tone for their success, which means your success. You're reassured that you've made the right hire, and they're excited to be part of an organization they can see themselves with for the long term.

Because here's the thing: Onboarding isn't just HR's role. It's also yours. HR may have paperwork and some structure for things every team member needs to know. However, the experience *you* create for your new hire in those first few days and weeks will shape how they see the role, the team, and the organization.

And you can absolutely do this without piling more onto your plate. In this chapter, we'll talk not just about your actions in the hiring process but also simple, practical ways to take ownership of onboarding and make it an easy, smooth, positive start for both you and your new team member. And I'll show you exactly how the framework can help you do that.

THE PAUSE-CONSIDER-ACT FRAMEWORK FOR BETTER HIRING

You can use the **Pause-Consider-Act** framework as a straightforward but powerful tool to guide every step of the hiring and onboarding process. It gives you a structured way to think about how you're creating roles, supporting candidates, and ensuring that you're balancing the dual needs to fill the role as quickly as possible while also making sure the candidate will enjoy it (instead of having "buyer's remorse").

Pause

The first step in the hiring process is to **Pause** before you jump into action. Think about what the role truly needs. You might be tempted to post the same job description you've been using for years or just start conducting interviews, but if you don't pause to reflect, you risk rushing into a process that may not lead to the best results—or candidate.

Ask yourself:

- Why is this role open?

- What are the most important skills or qualities that a new hire needs to succeed in this position?

- What challenges did the previous person in this role face, and why did they leave?

- What is the reality of the workload, environment, and work-life balance, and how can we communicate this honestly to candidates?

- How can we design interview questions to assess not just technical skills but also how they'd work with others?

- Whose input should we consider in the hiring process? Do they all need to be involved in interviews, or can we incorporate their questions in other ways?

- How can we ensure the hiring process feels like a two-way street, showing candidates we respect their time and effort throughout the experience?

- When deciding between strong candidates, what are the key priorities or qualities we should focus on to ensure the best fit for the team and organization?

- What's the best approach to celebrate the candidate we're offering the role to, while also showing respect to those who took the time to interview but weren't selected?

This same framework applies to the onboarding process. Once you've found the right candidate, pause again to ensure their first days and weeks set them—and you—up for success. Think about what your new hire needs to feel welcomed and prepared, and ask yourself:

- What will they need for their arrival?
- How can we make sure it's ready?
- What will their first day (and days) look like?
- Who should they meet, and how will we introduce them to the team?
- How can we give them clarity about their role while helping them feel supported as they settle in?

By taking the time to pause and think through these questions, you create a thoughtful, intentional process that helps your new hire feel valued, supported, and ready to succeed.

Consider

As you think through these questions, take into account both your organization's needs and the candidate's experience. Put yourself in their shoes: How will they perceive your company and the role? From the moment they apply, candidates are building an impression of your organization. Every e-mail, interaction, and step in the interview process shapes how they feel about the opportunity and whether they see your organization as a place they want to work.

Take a moment to consider the structure of your interview process. One often overlooked aspect is the number of interview rounds. While it may be tempting to schedule multiple rounds, this can quickly become frustrating and repetitive for candidates, especially if they're repeatedly asked the same questions. Instead of jumping in and using the "same as usual" approach, decide in advance how many rounds are truly necessary, what each round should achieve, and how to make the process as efficient as possible. Each interview round should build on the previous one, avoiding unnecessary repetition and showing candidates that you respect their time.

That sense of respect matters. Candidates are human—they want to feel they belong and are valued for who they are and what they can bring to the team. A simple yet powerful way to create that feeling is by telling them why you're interested in them for the role. Don't assume they know why they stood out—be specific. Was it their experience in a similar role? A fresh perspective they bring to the team? Let them know. It's not just about making them feel they're lucky to have a chance at the role; it's also about helping them see why they were chosen because of their unique qualities.

When designing the interview process, consider the candidate's experience from start to finish:

- **How many rounds of interviews are necessary?** Be mindful to avoid unnecessary repetition while ensuring each round builds on the last.

- **Are you asking the right questions?** Ensure that candidates aren't asked the same questions repeatedly and leave each interaction with clarity about the role and your organization.

- **How are you communicating and understanding more about their strengths?** Share specific feedback about why they were chosen to interview, and ask questions to truly understand how their skills and interests align with the role.

- **What's your team's process for differing opinions?** It's natural for team members to have varied impressions of candidates. Plan how to resolve these differences, whether through voting, weighing certain voices more heavily, or other methods. Also, think about how to communicate your final decisions to colleagues who may wonder why their feedback wasn't considered or differed from the eventual outcome.

This same approach carries into onboarding. Don't just ask yourself the following questions, but solicit your team's input as well, to create a welcoming, productive environment for the new hire:

- **What did your team like and what would they change about their onboarding? What does your team wish they'd known when they started?** You never know until you ask. You can use feedback on past onboarding experiences to identify improvements.

- **How can you take this feedback to build a better process moving forward?** Explain to your team that you want to know how to make onboarding smoother and more effective for new hires and for the existing team.

- **What shift or schedule makes sense for them to start?** Are there teammates they should shadow or learn from? Are there opportunities for them to observe, practice, and receive feedback?

By thoughtfully considering these elements of hiring and onboarding, you create a structured, respectful, and repeatable process that not only helps you find the right candidate but also ensures they feel valued and prepared when they start. During interviews, focus on finding the right fit by understanding not just skills but also how a candidate aligns with the team. Then, carry that same intentionality into onboarding. It's not just about handing over a checklist; it's also about creating an environment where new hires feel confident, valued, and ready to contribute, while ensuring the team feels supported and included in the process.

Act

After you **Pause** and **Consider**, the final step is to **Act**, which includes both how you conduct the interviews and how you onboard new hires. Acting involves being proactive and transparent throughout the process. This is your opportunity to set candidates up for success by giving them a clear and honest picture of the role, making decisions efficiently to move forward with confidence, and ensuring everything is ready to welcome them onto the team.

For the interview process, one of the most important actions is to use the job description as a marketing tool, to set clear expectations and responsibilities and avoid misalignment. A good job description should do more than list requirements and responsibilities— it should also attract the right candidates and filter out those for whom the role may not be a fit.

One note: We've talked about how, if certain aspects of the role are so challenging that they consistently drive candidates (or employees) away, it's a signal to pause and consider. But how do you act? That can mean, in the job description if possible, being honest about the realities of the position, including listing any key aspects like long hours, frequent travel, or high-pressure deadlines. This ensures candidates have a realistic understanding of what to expect and reduces the risk of them feeling misled once they start (perhaps texting their old boss on Day 1, asking for their old job back).

For example, if the role involves regularly dealing with frustrated customers, long hours at the end of the quarter to meet tight deadlines, or lower wages in a nonprofit setting balanced by the opportunity to make a meaningful impact on the mission, candidates deserve to know. If you try to hide those for the sake of getting them in the door, you'll likely be conducting another hiring process sooner rather than later (and likely read a negative review on a public employer review website soon). By setting clear expectations, you're not only protecting your new hire's experience but also building trust and creating an opportunity to identify ways to support your team in handling these realities effectively.

To further improve the hiring process, consider preparing a go-to list of interview questions. Having a list in advance ensures that every candidate is evaluated on the same criteria and helps streamline the process. It also lets you focus on asking what really matters, so you're making the best use of your time, and theirs, during interviews.

Here's a starter list of topics and sample interview questions you can standardize and expand on.

- **Role fit and motivation:**

  "What aspects of this role interest you the most, and why? Are there any parts you find less appealing? This isn't about judging—it's about ensuring the role is a good fit for you."

  – This gauges how well the role fits with their interests and gives insight into potential hesitations.

- **Skills and capabilities:**

  "This role has some skills that we need on Day 1, and others that can be learned over time. Some of those needed right away are [insert skills]. What is your experience in those to date?"

  "How would you approach [insert common scenarios in the role]?"

  – These help evaluate their experience and approach to critical tasks in the role.

- **Approach to challenges:**

  "This role involves [insert specific challenge, e.g., managing tight deadlines or working with cross-functional teams]. How have you handled similar challenges in the past, and how do you think you would approach them here?"

  – This assesses their ability to manage the specific challenges of the job and provides insight into their work style.

- **Collaboration and growth:**

  "Do you usually prefer working on your own or as part of a team? Can you share why and how that's worked for you in the past?"

"When you're working with a team, what's your approach to making sure everyone stays on the same page and gets things done?"

– These questions help assess their teamwork skills (which can vary based on the needs of the role), collaboration style, and how they approach building relationships with others.

Once you've created a set list of interview questions, gather input from your team members and other managers to incorporate questions they've found effective. Consider creating a shared guide or having a team member help compile one. This way, interviews feel less like starting from scratch every time. It ensures consistency across interviews, saves time, and creates a valuable resource for everyone involved (and if you do create this, remember to highlight it as a consideration in your performance review and encourage any team members working on it to do the same).

Acting in the Onboarding Process: How to Truly Set Your New Hire Up for Success

Let's talk about that first day. The onboarding process is your opportunity to help a new hire move from being an excited candidate to becoming an engaged team member. Ever heard the phrase "set someone up for success" and wondered what it really means? This is your chance to do exactly that. By taking thoughtful steps from the start, you not only make them feel welcome but also lay a strong foundation for them to understand what's expected, know what to do, and do it well. Here's how to make the onboarding experience smooth and impactful.

- **Prepare for Day 1: Create a welcoming first impression**

    Day 1 sets the tone for your new hire's experience, so make it a positive one. A thoughtful, organized first day can turn nervous energy into excitement and confidence. Have their workspace ready, whether it's a desk, equipment, or access to tools, and make sure everything is set up and tested before they arrive. Walking into a prepared space shows that you're excited to have them join. Plan personal introductions with the team that go beyond generic welcomes. You can add something meaningful about their role or background to make the connection genuine ("You'll work with Lisa on monthly reports—she has all sorts of hacks to get them done quickly, and she also makes the best chocolate chip cookies you've ever had"). Lastly, give them a schedule for the day so they know what to expect, whether it's meetings, a team lunch, or time to get settled (having time to complete any paperwork, so they don't have to take it home and do it then).

- **Develop and share a clear onboarding plan**

  A structured onboarding plan provides clarity and sets expectations for the first few weeks and months. Start with a detailed first week that includes orientation, shadowing sessions, and time to get familiar with tools and systems. Let them know who they can reach out to for questions. Set milestones for their first month that build confidence, like completing their first project or leading a small task. Extend the road map beyond the first month with opportunities for growth, such as owning responsibilities, collaborating across teams, or exploring training programs. This can vary by role, but having certainty can be especially welcome as a new hire.

- **Incorporate shadowing opportunities**

  Shadowing helps new hires learn their role and the team dynamics in a low-pressure way. Pair them with a co-worker to guide them through day-to-day processes and provide a go-to person for informal questions. Have them shadow you in a meeting or process. Encourage cross-team shadowing so they can see how other roles connect to their work and the broader organization. Before each shadowing session, make clear what's expected and what they can take out of it. After each shadowing session, schedule time for them to ask questions of the person they shadowed. This allows them to discuss what they observed, ask questions, and start applying what they learned.

- **Create opportunities for connection**

  Building relationships early fosters a sense of belonging. Go beyond "Day 1 introductions" by continuing to connect them with key teammates and colleagues over the first few weeks. Host a casual welcome event, like a team lunch, coffee chat, or virtual meet-and-greet, or even just highlight them and get their thoughts in a pre-shift team huddle to create a relaxed space for building connections.

- **Provide ongoing support and feedback**

  Onboarding doesn't end after the first week. Keep the momentum going with regular support and feedback that they can count on. Hold regular one-on-ones (whether an official meeting or quick conversation—more on these in the next chapter) to check in on progress, answer questions, and address any challenges. Use these sessions to provide feedback and recognize their contributions. Encourage them to ask questions, even if it's about things already covered. Reinforce that it's okay to ask again to make sure they're learning. Celebrate even seemingly small accomplishments to show their efforts are noticed and appreciated, helping them feel valued and motivated.

By taking these thoughtful steps, onboarding becomes more than a checklist or one-day event—it becomes a meaningful way to integrate your new hire into the team and set them up for long-term success. When you prioritize preparation, structure, connection, and support, you create an experience that benefits both your new hire and your organization.

And one more tip: To make onboarding sustainable, consider creating resources that can be reused and refined over time. Have team members (including new hires) contribute by developing guides or checklists that future hires can benefit from. Use screenshares during training sessions and record them (or record them as you or team members work independently) to build a library of helpful videos and tutorials. While every work environment is unique, pausing to think about what can be documented or streamlined helps make each onboarding experience easier and more valuable for everyone. The simple act of pausing, considering what's needed, and acting on those ideas can have a lasting impact on how smoothly new hires transition into their roles.

WHAT CANDIDATES WANT TO KNOW (BUT MIGHT NOT ASK)

Remember, candidates are people, too. They have real questions and concerns, but they might not bring them up because they don't want to be judged or risk losing the offer. I've been there myself, especially when I was interviewing for that in-house role. But those unspoken questions often play a big role in whether someone truly wants to accept the job. And if the role isn't the right fit, it's better to figure that out now than have them regret it later. Here are some of the things candidates often wonder about but might not feel comfortable asking:

- **Training and development:** What resources are available to help them succeed in the role? Is there structured onboarding, regular training, or opportunities to develop new skills? How will they be supported in their growth within the company?

- **Autonomy and support:** Will they have the ability to make decisions on their own with the support they need? For example, will they have regular one-on-one meetings with their manager (whether you or their direct manager) to discuss challenges and progress, or will they feel micromanaged? How much independence is expected versus collaboration?

- **Working hours and ability to disconnect after hours:** What are their working hours? How often will they be expected to work late or on their "off days"? Are they expected to respond to e-mails or calls after business hours, or is there a known expectation about responding the next business day (and is that actually supported)?

- **Workload and "busy periods":** How much work will they be expected to handle? Are there times of the year or specific tasks that lead to longer hours or higher stress levels?

- **Travel expectations:** If travel is a part of the role, how often will they be away, and what kind of travel will it be—day trips, overnights, or weeks away at a time?

- **Flexibility:** Is remote work an option? What kind of flexibility do they have around scheduling or time off?

- **Mistakes:** What happens if they make a mistake? Is there a culture of learning from errors, or will they feel punished? Are there systems in place to help them recover and improve, such as training sessions, shadowing, or coaching?

- **Performance evaluations and career growth:** How often are performance reviews held? What criteria will be used, and how can they grow in their role over time?

Proactively Provide Information

As a manager, you can take the pressure off—and make it their favorite interview ever—by sharing answers to these questions up front. Most candidates won't ask, even though these are the things that can make or break their experience. Bringing these up as a manager not only shows transparency but also builds trust from the beginning. How can you do that? With just a few simple words. For example, during the interview process, you might say, "I know work-life balance is important, so let me tell you a little about how we handle that here." Or, "You might be wondering about career growth—let me walk you through how promotions typically happen on our team."

As I'll emphasize throughout this book, involving your team in the process is key. You don't have to—and shouldn't—go it alone. Earlier, we talked about asking current employees for their honest feedback on their own hiring and onboarding experiences. The "honest" part is crucial, so make it clear by saying something like, "I'm asking to make sure we're supporting you and future hires." Find out what they liked and what they wish they had known earlier. Use this valuable input to refine and improve the process for future candidates.

Create No-Judgment Zones

Besides providing information, you can create opportunities for candidates to ask questions in a low-pressure, no-judgment environment. One way to do this is by having candidates meet informally with future peers, not just higher-ups. In these conversations, they can ask questions candidly, like what a typical day-to-day is like, what the team is like, whether the schedule or work-life balance is what's been portrayed, or how often they'll need to check in outside of normal working hours.

This approach gives candidates a clearer picture of what their day-to-day responsibilities might look like without the pressure of feeling like they're being evaluated (so make sure to communicate that the purpose of the interview is to ask any questions they'd like). It also ensures their questions about the role are addressed before they officially start, providing transparency into the realities of the job. Just make sure to pause and consider whether you're always asking the same team member to be the go-to peer interviewer. Rotating this responsibility can give others an opportunity to be involved in the hiring process while also giving that team member a likely needed break.

BETWEEN HIRING AND ONBOARDING

There's an important phase between "You're hired!" and "Welcome to your first day!" Before they start, take the time to reach out to your new team member personally. This doesn't mean giving them tasks or making them work before they've started (avoid the "I'll send you things to look over" trap). Instead, use this time to let them hear from you and possibly a few team members. A quick e-mail or message expressing your excitement about them joining the team can go a long way, because people don't just want to hear from HR with the formal documents. Hearing from their manager and team makes the experience more personal and shows that they're valued beyond the formalities of new hire paperwork. This simple gesture reinforces their decision to join your team and sets a positive tone even before their first day.

HIRING AND ONBOARDING: WHAT TO KEEP IN MIND

Feel free to jot down notes as you go, but my goal is to keep things simple and give you clear, doable next steps. This chapter covered a lot, so here are a few key takeaways to keep in mind:

1. **Ask your team about their experiences.** Gather honest feedback from your current employees about what worked in their hiring and onboarding process and anything they wish had been different. Use that to improve your current process, and then tell them what you're changing because of their feedback.

2. **Be intentional about your hiring and onboarding processes.** Create a consistent set of impactful questions for each role, ensuring all candidates are evaluated on the same criteria. Make a guide so it can be used in the future. This not only speeds up the process but also helps avoid unnecessary repetition across interview rounds.

3. **Involve team members in the hiring process— but ask first.** Not everyone has the capacity or interest to participate in interviewing. But if you involve some people and don't involve others, they'll likely feel left out, even if it's because you know or believe they're too busy. By asking who would like to be involved (and being clear with those who seem busy that you'd love to have them involved but don't want to add to their plates if they can't), you avoid making someone feel excluded. Remember I said that employees tend to fill in the gaps with the worst-case scenario? That means if you don't involve certain people, they may feel like they weren't included for a reason.

4. **Acknowledge that candidates see the job as a prize.** It's natural for candidates to be excited, but remind them (and yourself and your team) that it's a two-way street. They're evaluating you as much as you're evaluating them.

5. **Proactively share key information.** Don't wait for candidates to ask about working hours, the ability to disconnect after hours, travel expectations, flexibility, or career growth—offer that information up front.

6. **Create opportunities for candid conversations.** Encourage candidates to meet with team members in informal settings where they can ask questions and get real answers without feeling judged.

7. **Tell candidates why they stood out.** Don't assume they know why you chose to interview them or why you choose to extend them the offer. Be specific about what made them a great fit. Have you ever had a job where a boss proactively told you this? Most of us haven't—but you can. It will make their day (and likely longer).

8. **Set up a thoughtful Day 1 experience.** Ensure the basics are ready before the new hire arrives—like their workspace, access to tools, and introductions to the team. A well-prepared first day helps them feel welcomed and valued from the start.

9. **Create a clear onboarding road map.** Provide a structured plan that outlines what they'll focus on during their first week, month, and beyond. Include opportunities to shadow teammates, learn key systems, and gain clarity about their role and responsibilities. This gives them confidence and sets them up for success.

REMEMBER THIS

Using the **Pause-Consider-Act** framework helps you create a hiring and onboarding process that's transparent, supportive, and human. Remember, candidates want to feel like they belong, not just that they've won a job. And as a manager, it's your job to create that sense of belonging from the start. By pausing to reflect, considering the candidate's perspective, and acting with transparency and empathy, you'll set both your new hires and your organization up for actual, realistic success.

Questions for Self-Reflection

- **How do I currently set expectations during the hiring process?**

  Think about whether you're being fully transparent with candidates about the role, workload, and team dynamics. Are there areas where you can offer more clarity up front?

- **Do I involve my team in the hiring process, and how can I improve that involvement?**

  Consider whether your current team is part of the interview process or onboarding experience. What input or role can they contribute to help new hires feel welcomed and informed?

- **Am I taking time to reflect on past employees who left and why they did (including because of the demands of the role or misalignment)?**

  Reflect on whether you've analyzed turnover reasons and made adjustments based on feedback. Are you learning from experiences to improve the hiring process?

- **Do my onboarding processes make new hires feel welcome and set up for short- and long-term success?**

  Take a minute to consider whether you're giving new hires the tools and support they need to hit the ground running. Are you helping them feel like part of the team from Day 1 and making sure they're truly prepared for what's ahead?

- **What would my team say about our onboarding process, and how can I ask them?**

  Have you ever directly asked your team for feedback on your onboarding? It can be eye-opening to hear their thoughts about what works and where things could improve. It's important they explain why, so try to get their honest input.

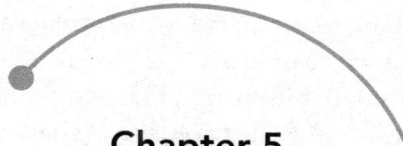

Chapter 5

Meetings That Move Things Forward (Not Waste Time)

I'll never forget the first time I heard someone say, "This meeting could've been an e-mail." You can probably imagine exactly the voice they said it in (and what their face looked like). It was during a project meeting with multiple departments, where we'd spent an hour listening to one person giving an update that could have been written in a few bullet points. The rest of us just sat there, nodding along, waiting for it to end. No one really needed to speak, no one gave feedback, and no one asked any questions. As we all shuffled out, someone muttered, "Well, that was a waste of time," and I couldn't help but agree, because this wasted hour likely meant I'd be working an extra hour that night with my laptop cracked open on my couch.

It got me thinking: Should we cancel these types of meetings altogether and just rely on e-mail updates? What's the point of meeting if it's not helping anyone?

But canceling all meetings isn't the answer. Sure, we've all been in meetings that feel pointless, but meetings done right can be incredibly powerful. The problem isn't the meeting itself—it's the structure, the timing, and the lack of purpose. As a manager, you need to be especially aware of, and intentional, about this because your team is looking to you to make their time valuable.

It's not just about team meetings; I've also seen the impact of poorly managed smaller meetings, like one-on-ones. I once had a boss who was consistently late to ours. We'd have a regular 30-minute meeting scheduled, and I'd sit there awkwardly waiting, signing out and then back in "just in case," until they finally showed up, usually at least 15 minutes late. They'd apologize, explaining that they were stuck in a meeting with a senior executive, and then ask if I could "run over" to make up the time. But I couldn't do that—at least not by letting down other people the same way I'd felt let down myself. I had other meetings lined up, so I'd scramble to rearrange my day, feeling frustrated and unable to push back because, after all, it was the boss.

Now, while emergencies happen, especially at higher levels, when your team members feel like they're constantly being ditched for someone higher up in the org chart, it sends a message that they don't matter. As a manager, you need to show up for your team, and that means respecting their time as much as you possibly can. If something unavoidable comes up, it's okay to reschedule, but don't make it a habit. And if you're in a meeting with someone else, let them know you've committed to meeting with a team member and you want to model showing up on time for your team. That kind of respect and modeling behavior speaks volumes, and it makes your life easier by being able to reliably provide your team members the support they need.

THE TRAP OF OPEN-DOOR POLICIES

Open-door policies often sound great in theory—they imply you're approachable, and your team can come to you anytime they need help or advice. But in practice, an open-door policy without scheduled time to meet regularly can quickly become a burden for everyone involved.

Picture this: You're deep in a project, trying to meet a deadline, when suddenly there's a knock at the door. Then another knock—because someone else is right behind them. Or maybe it's three different pings in your Teams chat from team members who need to ask questions because they don't have designated time with you. Before you know it, your focus is wiped out, and you're trying to think clearly and give help to these "quick questions" when you've completely lost your train of thought with what you were working on.

What's the solution? Regular, structured meetings. When your team knows they have dedicated one-on-one time with you, they won't feel such a need to interrupt your day with small, nonurgent issues. And you'll have a better sense of their workload, challenges, and needs without being interrupted.

It's common for managers to think, *Well, if they need me, they'll come to me*, but the reality is your team members might *not* feel comfortable interrupting you or bringing up an issue unless it feels urgent—or when it's too late. This approach can lead to situations where small problems snowball into bigger ones because there was never a clear time to address them. As a manager, you're neither a mind reader nor an octopus with eight arms able to handle everything. But your team members don't know that, so you have to give them a peek into what you're working on and give them time when they know they can get your dedicated attention. This is when team members can come to you and feel like their concerns matter. You'll have a much better handle on what's going on, and they'll feel more supported knowing they have time set aside for them.

MEETINGS DON'T HAVE TO MEAN THE CONFERENCE ROOM

One of the biggest misconceptions about meetings is that they always need to be in a formal conference room with a set agenda and an hour on the clock. In reality, the most effective meetings don't always look like that, especially depending on your industry or the makeup of your team.

If you're working in health care, manufacturing, or retail, your meetings might take the form of pre- or post-shift huddles. These could be three- to five-minute quick check-ins where everyone aligns on the day's priorities and addresses any concerns. They don't require a long, drawn-out session, but they do need focus and structure to ensure everyone understands what they need to know and has the opportunity to add input.

For teams that work remotely or across different time zones, you may not be able to hold regular, real-time meetings. In those cases, asynchronous communication methods like shared documents or video updates can be incredibly effective. Each team member can contribute in their own time, ensuring no one is left out because the meeting time doesn't work for them.

The key is to adapt your meeting style to the needs of your team. Not all meetings need to be an hour-long sit-down session. Consider what your team needs: Are you all in the same location or spread across multiple time zones? Do you need to huddle quickly before or after a shift? Can a brief check-in or shared update get the job done more effectively? The goal is to make meetings meaningful, efficient, and tailored to how your team works best. But effective meetings aren't just about planning; they're also about how you engage with your team during them. This is where active listening becomes essential.

Active Listening: It's Not What You Think It Is

You might think you know what active listening is—nodding along, making the right sounds of agreement, maybe even summarizing what your team member said at the end of their statement. But active listening is so much more than that. It's the key to showing your team that you're fully engaged—or making it clear when you're not.

If you're meeting with someone in person and your eyes are darting around the room, or you keep glancing at your watch or phone, it sends a message that your team picks up on—that you're not fully present. Even if you tell yourself it's just for a second, your team notices—and those brief moments of distraction can have a bigger impact than you might think. There may be times when you need to keep an eye on your phone, especially in case of an emergency. But if you're checking it out of habit, that quick glance can make them feel like you're bored, disinterested, or simply don't value what they're saying.

In virtual meetings, it can be even more tempting to multitask, but it's even more obvious when you do it. If you have a second monitor and you're glancing at it the whole time, or if you're muted and not engaged, it's incredibly easy for your team to lose trust. They might think, *If my manager doesn't care enough to pay attention now, how invested are they in my work overall?* Over time, these small actions can erode trust and make team members hesitant to share openly, thinking their concerns or contributions aren't a priority. Staying present—no matter what the situation—shows respect, builds trust, and encourages meaningful communication.

And yes, you're human, and there will be times when exceptions are necessary. Transparency and communication can make all the difference, especially in building trust. If you're expecting an important message, let your team know up front. For example, say, "I might need to check my phone briefly during this meeting; I'm waiting on a call from a family member, but I'm fully here with you otherwise." This small heads-up reassures them that your attention isn't divided because you're not interested, but due to a situation outside your control.

For neurodivergent individuals (such as those with ADHD, autism, or sensory processing differences), this approach can be especially valuable. If you need to fidget, take notes, or step away briefly to focus, sharing that up front can help normalize different ways of staying present. You don't need to share anything you're not comfortable with, but it can be helpful to add a brief explanation, such as, "Sometimes I need to do X to stay focused, but I'm fully engaged in what we're discussing."

It also lets your team feel comfortable managing their needs without feeling like they have to hide them. For example, if you set the tone that it's okay to check their phone for something important, they won't feel like they have to tell their sick child not to call because they're in a meeting with the boss. Let them know it's fine to glance at their phones for urgent matters or share what helps them stay focused, without worrying about upsetting you. Creating that kind of understanding builds trust and makes it easier for everyone to work together in a way that feels natural and supportive.

Active listening is about being fully present, which means putting aside distractions and focusing on the person in front of you. This is especially important to keep in mind when planning and leading meetings as a manager. It's one of the simplest yet most effective ways to show that you respect their time and value their input. When you actively listen, you create a space where they feel heard, understood, and encouraged to share openly, all actions that can help your team perform at their best.

"I'm Too Busy": How Meetings Can Actually Help Your Team Save Time

You're not the only one who might feel overwhelmed by meetings. Another challenge that often comes up about meetings, especially one-on-ones, is that your team may feel like *they're* just too busy to take time for these discussions. They may be juggling multiple projects or dealing with high-pressure deadlines and see the meeting as just another thing on their already overflowing to-do list.

However, when your team members are overwhelmed, meeting with them shouldn't just be another check-the-box obligation, but an opportunity to help them strategize and prioritize. If someone is feeling buried under their workload, they may not have the headspace to step back and think strategically about how they're spending their time. That's where you come in as a manager. Use your one-on-ones to help them pause, reflect on what's on their plate, and find ways to make their work more efficient. In other words, spend time to save time.

For example, if a team member is struggling to balance a client project with internal responsibilities, you can help them figure out what can be delegated, where they can streamline processes, or how they can adjust timelines to make things more manageable. Often, people just need an outside perspective to help them see where adjustments can be made. In the long run, these meetings don't need to be a time drain; instead, they're a way to make sure your team is working efficiently and not burning out.

Meetings as Investments

Think of your meetings as an investment in your team's success. Time and energy are two of the most precious resources at work, and when you schedule a meeting, you're spending both (especially if you start adding up the costs of everyone's pay during that meeting). That's why it's important to ensure your meetings serve a clear purpose and deliver value to everyone involved. Are you using your one-on-one meetings to get to know and understand your team members? Are your team meetings moving projects forward? Are they giving your team the support they need to work more effectively? Or are they draining time and energy that could be better spent elsewhere?

Every meeting is an opportunity to invest in your team's development, alignment, and problem-solving. When you approach meetings with this mindset, you can start to see how even a short, well-structured check-in can save hours of confusion down the line. When meetings are done right, they clear the path for more productive work afterward. But if they're handled poorly, they can feel like an endless drain on everyone's energy.

MEETINGS THAT WORK: PAUSE-CONSIDER-ACT

Using the **Pause-Consider-Act** framework can help ensure your meetings are effective and purposeful. It's all about stopping to think about the structure, content, and timing of your meetings.

Pause

Take a step back and assess your current meetings. Are they too frequent? Too far apart? Are you meeting with no real purpose? Look at your schedule and figure out where things might need to be adjusted. If you find your team members constantly knocking on your door or sending chat messages because they don't have scheduled time with you, it's a sign you might need more regular time with your team members.

Consider

Think about the purpose of each meeting. What are you trying to accomplish? For one-on-ones, the goal might be to check in on progress, provide feedback, or support your team member's development. Team meetings could include brainstorming, decision-making, or updates. Be clear about what each meeting is for, and make sure your team knows what's expected of them. Also, consider their perspective—do they feel like they're too busy for the meeting? Are they feeling overwhelmed and just need more structure? Or do they feel like you already know everything and don't see the need to communicate details? Consider these angles and adjust your approach accordingly—and remember that if you fear "overcommunicating," that rarely happens. It's more often the opposite, and team members would love to hear more from you.

Act

Implement changes that make your meetings more structured and intentional. Use shared agendas to help your team prepare, and make sure you're prepared, too. Show up on time, be present, and make sure your team walks away with clear action items. For example, if you're setting up a one-on-one, include questions about workload, challenges, and opportunities for growth. Make these meetings actionable by leaving each one with the next steps for both you and your team members. Let them know their concerns have been heard, and show them how you're going to support them moving forward.

IDEAS FOR SHAKING UP MEETINGS

When meetings feel stale or unproductive, it's a sign something needs to change. Sometimes, adjusting the format or adding a creative element can make a big difference in boosting your team's engagement. One approach that's worked for me is having team members take turns explaining what they think someone else's job is like—it's a way to spark conversation and build understanding.

I did this once when I was leading a training for a team within a large organization that had undergone significant changes. Their leader was looking to reset and refocus on working collaboratively while helping the team adapt to the transitions. The team worked together pretty closely and thought they knew everything about each other's day-to-day. So, I asked two people with different roles on the team to describe what the other person's job was. The first person tried to explain their colleague's role and started stumbling and then laughing. It quickly turned into a game of telephone, where they realized they had no idea how to describe what the other person actually did. It was a lighthearted way to open up a conversation, but it also highlighted how little we sometimes know about what our colleagues are working on, even when we work closely together.

By having team members explain what they think others do, you create an opportunity for learning and empathy. People get to see the bigger picture of how different roles fit together, and it opens up conversations about how to collaborate more effectively. This type of exercise is also a great way to shake up internal meetings and make them more interactive.

Another way to make meetings more engaging is to give someone the chance to share a challenge they're facing and get input from teammates in different roles. For example, in a health care team meeting, a nurse might share how they've been feeling overwhelmed when dealing with anxious patients and family members during busy shifts. A colleague in administration might suggest using a specific kind phrase they've found helpful, like, "I understand this can be overwhelming, but you're in good hands, and we'll take care of you." Sharing those words could be helpful for other team members (and those patients and family members), but it might never come to light without intentionally creating an opportunity for it to be shared. These kinds of discussions not only provide practical solutions but also highlight how a supportive word or action can improve both patient care and team morale. It's a reminder that everyone has insights to share, and even a simple idea can make a meaningful impact.

As you work on shaking up your meetings to make them more engaging and useful, you might think about adjusting attendee lists. Yes, trimming the list can help keep things focused, but be careful. Like I mentioned back in Chapter 4, one of the trickiest parts of being a manager is dealing with team members feeling left out. People might complain about meetings (though hopefully not yours after using these tips), but being uninvited from or left off a meeting invitation can send an unintended message. You might be doing it to streamline the audience or save them time. But people tend to assume the worst, so they're more likely to wonder, *What did I do?* or *Do they not like my work . . . or me?* Before removing someone from a meeting or leaving them off an invite, think about how it might land, especially if it feels like someone else is getting more access or face time. When in doubt, explain your reasoning and give them the context. Sometimes, just knowing why makes all the difference. And if they still want to be there, consider letting them attend or at least making it optional so they feel respected, not sidelined.

MEETINGS WITH OTHER DEPARTMENTS OR GROUPS

Another way to energize your meetings is by creating opportunities for positive interaction with other departments or groups (such as different locations if your organization has different branches). Teams often only come together when their different members are working together on a project, but those situations don't always lead to meaningful relationship-building or knowledge-sharing. If people don't feel connected, it's easy for things to slide into "us versus them" territory. Suddenly it's harder to get on the same page, and even small misunderstandings can snowball. People start feeling frustrated, disconnected, or worse—judging each other based on one or two tough moments, or even just on what they've heard from others.

Consider setting up regular cross-departmental (or cross-location) meetings where teams can meet, learn about each other's workflows, and discuss challenges they face. These meetings can help break down silos and give your team a broader perspective on how the organization functions. It's also a great opportunity for professional development, as your team members can learn from the experiences and expertise of others outside their immediate circle.

For example, if you're leading a marketing team, organizing a meeting with the product or sales teams can provide valuable insights into how other parts of the organization operate and the challenges they face. Or create opportunities for field employees to connect with those at corporate headquarters. There are plenty of combinations and options, and each can be far more valuable than meeting only with your own team. These meetings don't have to be formal or lengthy—a 30-minute conversation can go a long way in creating greater understanding and better collaboration.

Additionally, consider offering these opportunities not just for you as a manager or other leaders to speak but also to hear from employees whose voices aren't always heard. Remember that it can feel intimidating for someone who hasn't spoken much in a "public" setting. So, before the meeting, take time to talk them through it, make sure they feel comfortable, and help them prepare. This creates an inclusive environment where team members at any level can contribute meaningfully and learn from each other.

RETHINKING MEETINGS FOR EFFICIENCY AND IMPACT

Take a step back and really rethink your meetings from every angle. Are they happening too often? Not enough? Do they have a clear purpose, or are they just on the calendar out of habit? Think about what your team actually needs: Could some updates be shared in an e-mail? Would a quick huddle or a more focused session work better? When you start being intentional about the frequency, structure, and content of your meetings, you'll see a real difference in how productive and meaningful they become.

Consider balancing the timing and structure of your meetings based on the needs of your colleagues. For example, if you have team members in different time zones, rotate meeting times periodically to ensure that no one group is always forced to attend outside their regular hours. Similarly, if your team includes employees working in shifts or on the road, adjust your approach to make meetings more accessible, whether through quick huddles or asynchronous updates when needed. These changes can help groups of employees from constantly feeling like "the other."

Think carefully about the content of your meetings as well. Are you defaulting to asking, "What's new?" with no clear focus? If so, it's no surprise meetings can feel aimless or unproductive. Instead, prepare a list of specific questions or topics to guide the conversation, such as:

- What's a current challenge you're facing?
- What's a recent success you're proud of?
- What feedback do you need from me or the team?

These types of questions don't just provide a structure that shows you're prepared but also create opportunities for meaningful conversations. They encourage problem-solving, recognition, and collaboration, making meetings more engaging and valuable for everyone involved. By tailoring both the timing and the content of your meetings, you create a more inclusive and effective space for communication.

When you have that space, what else should you share? As a manager, it's natural to want to keep your team informed and in the loop. That's a good thing. Even when your organization sends an all-employee e-mail, it can be helpful to talk about it in your meetings. It ensures your team understands the context, gives them a chance to ask questions, and helps connect the dots between organizational updates and them personally.

So, what about when you've got information to share with your team? Whether you need to or just want to, part of your job is figuring out what's worth sharing and how to share it in a way that works. Transparency is important, but it's just as important to make sure what you share is relevant and actionable for your team. Dumping everything on them—especially details they can't change or problems they can't fix—can cause unnecessary stress and leave them feeling overwhelmed.

Instead, focus on delivering information in a way that's clear, helpful, and empowering. Ask yourself: *Will this help my team do their jobs better? Does this information provide clarity or actionable steps?* If the answer is no, consider holding it back or reframing it to focus on what they need to know. For example, you can share updates about a new company initiative by explaining how it impacts their work rather than going into unnecessary details about how the executives made the decision (as tempting as that can be).

Balancing what to share and what to hold back isn't about keeping secrets—it's about communicating in a way that supports your team without piling on more than they can handle. By sharing what's most relevant and framing it in a way that resonates, you ensure your meetings stay focused, productive, and impactful.

USING AI FOR MEETING STRUCTURE AND IDEAS

If you're feeling stuck when it comes to planning meetings or just need a fresh way to kick things off, AI tools can be a great resource for brainstorming or creating agendas. Many organizations already offer access to different tools, but it's important to use them wisely— always follow your organization's policies, and don't include any names, sensitive information, or internal details. AI can't replace your judgment or experience, but when you're low on time or just need a jump start, it can help you come up with creative prompts, questions, or discussion ideas to make your meetings more engaging and useful.

If you're new to AI tools (like ChatGPT, and plenty of others that exist already, and more that are being developed every day), don't worry—it's never too late to start. I've shown friends and leaders how to use them, walking through the steps together, and they're almost always blown away. Without fail, I'll hear back a few days later: "Why didn't I know about this sooner?!" The good news is, using these tools is usually pretty straightforward. You just type in a request (or "prompt"), and it gives you ideas to work with. From there, you can tweak or build on those ideas using follow-up prompts to make them even more relevant to what you need.

What's a "Prompt"?

A prompt is simply what you type into the AI tool to tell it what you're looking for. Think of it like asking a question or giving instructions. It could be as simple as:

- "Can I have three intro questions* for a new hire meeting?"
- "Help me explain how to approach performance feedback to a new team member so it helps them, but doesn't upset them."
- "Can you suggest agenda ideas for a project kickoff?"

AI gives you a starting point. You can go back and ask additional prompts to tweak the output and make the ideas more relevant to your situation, but you're in the driver's seat. You decide what works and can (and should) adjust it to your voice and approach. It's like having a brainstorming partner on demand.

How Do You "Manage" AI?

Think of AI the same way you'd manage a new team member.** It can help you, but it's not perfect, and it doesn't replace your expertise. You need to:

---

* I like to call them "intro questions'" instead of "icebreakers"—you'll quickly find as a manager (if you haven't already) that not everyone's a fan of the word *icebreaker*.

** Yes to *thinking* that way. But please don't actually call AI your new team member—people really don't like that.

- Give clear instructions (your prompts).

- Double-check the output.

- Adjust (or ask additional prompts) what doesn't fit.

- Decide what gets used and what doesn't.

AI can help with a lot of things beyond meetings, such as brainstorming talking points, exploring how to approach tough conversations, thinking through how to be "strategic" when there's not much time, or even practicing what to say when you're stuck.

It can also help you look at the bigger picture of how you work. You can use AI to summarize meeting notes or transcripts so you're not scrambling to remember action items or decisions. You can even use it to review your calendar, asking prompts like "Does how I'm spending my time reflect my top priorities as a manager?" And for those meetings and conversations you overthink (because we all do), AI can help you run through different ways to approach them, helping you practice what to say so you feel more confident and prepared.

But just like with your team, your human approach is what matters most. AI can give suggestions, but your experience, tone, and judgment are what actually build trust and drive results. In the age of AI, people still want to feel human—and that includes working with leaders who show up as humans, too.

What Should You Keep in Mind?

A few important reminders about AI:

- Always follow your organization's policies for using AI tools. Some workplaces have specific guidelines or approved platforms, so make sure you're using them the right way.

- Be careful with confidentiality. Most AI models, especially public ones, learn from the prompts they receive. You shouldn't share your organization's name, internal details, personal information, or anything confidential. Stick to general language that helps you but still protects privacy.

- It's not a fact-checker or a dictionary. Be careful using it for anything that requires verified, accurate information—just ask the lawyers who've gotten in real trouble in court for using fake case citations AI made up. But for the tips in this book, you're not using it for hard facts. You're using it for ideas, talking points, or different ways to approach a situation, which AI can be perfect for.

- It's a helper, not a decision-maker. It can help you think through what to do or say, but your expertise, approach, and judgment always lead the way. When used thoughtfully, AI can be a great shortcut to get unstuck, save time, and approach situations, conversations, and meetings with more confidence.

To show how it can help with meetings specifically, here are some AI prompt examples (plus follow-up prompts) you can use to plan and run more effective meetings with your team.

"What are three questions I can ask in a one-on-one meeting to help support my team member's long-term professional development?"

- Follow-Up Prompts:
  - **"What are some ways I can make sure I align those goals with the needs of our team or organization?"**

    This helps focus on not just the employee's growth but also how it ties into the broader team or organizational objectives, making the development more meaningful and applicable.

- "Can you provide examples of actionable feedback I can give my team member during our one-on-one meetings to guide them both short term and for their long-term progress?"

  This prompt helps ensure you can offer specific, helpful feedback that leads to improvement now and keeps the employee on track.

- "What are three ways I can encourage my team members to take ownership of their development goals and track their progress?"

  This encourages employees to take initiative in their growth and promotes accountability and owning their career.

"What are strategies for balancing input from team members in different time zones during virtual meetings?"

- Follow-Up Prompts:

  - "How can I ensure team members in different time zones feel equally heard in decision-making and not left out?"

    This helps create opportunities for all team members to contribute, no matter their schedule. And it helps avoid unintentional hurt feelings if team members aren't included in meetings with others (even if you're doing so to help them).

  - "What tools can I use to collect feedback asynchronously from team members across time zones?"

    This helps you capture thoughts from everyone, without just having a bunch of different meetings at different times.

– "How do I handle follow-up with team members who couldn't attend the virtual meeting because of time zone differences?"

This keeps everyone in the loop and ensures nothing gets lost when someone can't attend.

"Give me three creative ideas for getting all team members to participate during a virtual team meeting."

- Follow-Up Prompts:

    – "What if my team doesn't normally like traditional team-building activities?"

    If this is true for your team, this prompt can help you meet them where they are and create moments that feel genuine, not forced.

    – "What if we're in the [insert] industry?"

    Adapting strategies to your specific industry helps your approach be practical and relevant to the team's real work.

    – "How can I adjust these for an in-person meeting?"

    This helps tailor ideas for face-to-face interactions, if you'll be meeting as a group.

AI can take some of the pressure off when you're trying to come up with fresh ways to engage your team. It's not about replacing your perspective; it's about giving you a tool to use your voice more effectively. This is how follow-up prompts can tweak the output to be more applicable to you, and even sound more like you. You can also carry this approach into the last chapter's ideas, like using AI to come up with great interview questions or creative onboarding ideas. And the same goes for other parts of this book. It's all about making it easier to show up as the leader you want to be.

TURNING MEETINGS INTO ACTION

No matter who's in the room, make sure every meeting ends with clear next steps and that everyone walks away knowing what they're responsible for and what to expect from others. For quick huddles, that may just mean saying them out loud (but remember that some people learn better by seeing it in writing, so using a bulletin board, e-mail recap, or other format can help ensure messages are truly understood).

For office environments, you may have access to AI meeting tools, which can help record and summarize notes for you (but still need human review to make sure they're accurate). If not, for one-on-one meetings, using a shared agenda can help track follow-ups and responsibilities, making it easy to revisit key points in future discussions.

For team meetings, ensure everyone understands, agrees with, and has access to the notes, even if they're assigned to someone during the meeting (just be sure to rotate the responsibility so it doesn't always fall on one person). Clear, shared notes ensure everyone heard the same thing and eliminate confusion about next steps. Summarize key takeaways, assign tasks, and confirm who's responsible for what, to avoid the classic game of telephone I mentioned earlier in the chapter. This approach ensures your meetings don't just end, but they also create momentum and accountability that are easy to track.

And speaking of keeping the momentum going, short surveys can be a powerful tool to keep things moving forward. Imagine you're in a meeting where you're asked to make an important decision on the spot. You're given the information right there, but what if you realize something later or wish you had more time to think? It can feel rushed, and you might end up giving input without fully considering the implications. That's where surveys—or opportunities for information and input (they don't have to be formal)—come in handy.

By sending out a quick survey before the meeting, you can gather input and give people time to think about the topic ahead of time. This allows everyone to come prepared and ready to discuss ideas thoughtfully. It's **Pause-Consider-Act** in action. If it's a big decision, consider using one meeting to review the input and talk it through, and then follow up in a later meeting (or meetings) to finalize the decision. This approach takes the pressure off, encourages more thoughtful contributions, and ensures that decisions are well-informed. Plus, post-meeting surveys can help you assess whether the process worked or whether adjustments are needed for next time.

Effective Meetings: What to Keep in Mind

To make sure you have actionable steps, here are key takeaways that make your meetings more effective, whether they're one-on-one or with your entire team:

1. **Schedule (and show up on time for) regular one-on-ones.** Set up recurring one-on-ones with each of your team members, whether it's weekly or biweekly. Use shared agendas so both of you can prepare in advance, ensuring time is spent efficiently.

2. **Respect time zones.** If your team is spread across different time zones, rotate meeting times so one group isn't always sacrificing their normal hours. For teams that can't meet in real time, use shared documents or asynchronous video updates.

3. **Prepare with purpose.** For both one-on-one and team meetings, use a shared document to outline the agenda in advance. This allows everyone to prepare, prevents surprises, and keeps the meeting focused.

4. **Shorten meetings where possible.** Don't assume that every meeting needs to be an hour long. Try cutting your meetings down to 20 to 30 minutes and focus on a few key topics. This forces

everyone to get to the point quickly and avoids
unnecessary discussions.

5. **Communicate clearly, but don't overwhelm.**
    Be intentional about what you share during
    meetings. Be honest with your team, but
    avoid overwhelming them with details they
    can't control. If you're facing challenges that
    don't impact their day-to-day work, focus
    on the actions they can take and how you'll
    support them.

6. **Follow up with action items.** After each
    meeting, send a brief summary with clear
    action items. For one-on-ones, this could be a
    simple list of tasks or decisions made. For team
    meetings, make sure everyone understands their
    responsibilities and deadlines.

Meetings are more than just a way to share information. They're
a way to show up for your team and to give them the time and attention they need to succeed. Whether it's a formal one-on-one, a
quick huddle, or a team brainstorming session, the way you handle
meetings sets the tone for your team's engagement and productivity.

So, show up. Be present. And make every meeting matter.

Questions for Self-Reflection

- **Do I schedule enough one-on-one meetings with my team members?**

  Reflect on whether your team has regular opportunities to meet with you and discuss their challenges, progress, and goals in a structured way.

- **Are my meetings focused and purposeful, or do they feel like a waste of time?**

  Consider whether your meetings are driving action and clarity, or whether they could be more efficient or streamlined.

- **How do I accommodate different working styles or time zones in my meetings?**

  Think about whether your meetings are accessible to all team members, regardless of their location or schedule, and whether you're creating space for everyone to participate.

- **Are my team meetings truly impactful, or could they be adjusted?**

  Reflect on whether your meetings are driving value or just taking up time. Are you focusing on the right topics? Is everyone walking away clear on the next steps, or are there ways you could shake things up?

- **How could I use quick surveys between meetings to gather feedback and improve?**

  Consider using short surveys between meetings to gather ideas and input from your team. It's an easy way to get feedback so you can discuss it in the meeting rather than put them on the spot.

Chapter 6

Delegation

How to Stop Doing Everything Yourself

In Chapter 5, I mentioned that you might feel like you're expected to be an octopus with eight arms to juggle everything. Or you might feel like you're expected to be a wizard to somehow find 36 hours in a day to get everything done. The pressure to handle everything yourself? It's real. You're juggling a thousand tasks, pulled in every direction, and still trying to hold it all together. And yet, despite the chaos, there's one word most managers avoid: *delegation*. You're not alone. Managers often tell me, "I know I *should* delegate, but it's a lot harder to do in real life. So, I don't." Does this ring a bell? You might tell yourself it'll take *too long* to explain the task, or you worry that it won't be done *right*. Maybe you enjoy some tasks even though you know they aren't the best use of your time. You might even worry about no longer being seen as needed if you start handing off too much work. Or you feel guilty, thinking your team is already overloaded, so they'll just quit if you give more work to do. Whatever your reason, the end result is the same: feeling overworked, overwhelmed, and as if you're constantly falling behind.

This isn't just anecdotal. According to Gallup research, the stress levels of managers are significantly higher than those of individual contributors.[1] Why is that? Managers who feel overwhelmed by unmanageable workloads or constant time pressure experience increased levels of stress, anxiety, and even burnout. The constant need to balance expectations while navigating the daily demands of leadership leaves little time to focus on higher-level strategic thinking. When you try to take on too much without delegating, it doesn't just affect your productivity, but it also impacts your mental well-being and your ability to lead effectively. And this stress inevitably trickles down to the rest of the team.

It's critical to remember that delegation isn't just about lightening your load in the short term; it's also about creating opportunities for your team members to grow in the long term. Encouraging your team to try new things is a vital part of their development, but they need to feel supported to take on new responsibilities. This means providing clear guidance, making space for questions, and offering constructive feedback, especially when things don't go perfectly. When team members feel like they can ask for help without judgment and learn from their mistakes, they're more likely to step up and take on new challenges, certainly more so than if they try them and are then met with a frustrated sigh or no feedback at all. The key is creating an environment where they want to try again, knowing they'll get the support they need to succeed.

HOLDING ON OUT OF FEAR

Let's start with a scenario that probably sounds familiar. John, an experienced manager, had been handling a set of reports for years. At first, he took them on because he was good at it and he enjoyed having a project that he could control and format exactly the way he liked. Over time, these reports became his "thing." Everyone in the company knew John for producing great reports, and it felt good to be known for doing something so well. As his team grew and his managerial responsibilities increased, he found himself increasingly frustrated with the endless stream of "people" issues that arose. The unpredictability of managing others left him feeling exhausted, but he always found comfort in his reports—a steady, reliable task that he could tackle independently and easily, free from the unpredictable nature of interpersonal challenges.

Even on vacation, John would log in to complete the reports. It didn't matter that his "real job" was managing people—he convinced himself no one else could handle those reports quite like he could. His sense of responsibility toward them had grown so strong that he always made time for them, even if it meant stepping away from family time.

Here's the interesting part: John complained about the reports constantly. He didn't like how they ate into his personal time or added to his duties. Yet, when the chance to delegate them came up, he always hesitated. His team members would even offer to help, suggesting he finally take a real vacation without worrying about work. But John declined, saying, "It's really no big deal," even though his kids didn't agree as they waited for him to finish his reports before they could head to the beach.

The reports had become more than just a task for John—they had become a symbol of his reliability and value to the company. They were his security blanket. Letting go of them felt like letting go of a part of his identity. What would he be known for if he wasn't the guy who did the reports? He worried he'd lose the sense of importance that came with owning that responsibility.

It's a common trap managers fall into: Tasks feel like markers of your worth, and the thought of handing them off creates a sense of uncertainty. The truth is that hoarding work not only creates burnout but also stifles the growth of the team. If you don't delegate, your team won't have the chance to develop new skills and take on more responsibility. You need to do it. You need to delegate. It takes trusting your team—and trusting yourself to let go.

WHY DELEGATION MATTERS

Delegation, at its core, is built on trust—trusting your team to handle tasks and trusting yourself to let go of control. Without trust, delegation simply doesn't work. When team members fear making mistakes and getting in trouble, they'll hesitate to work independently, let alone try something new. Even *with* trust, successful delegation requires careful planning and clear communication. If you're thinking,

This sounds like too much work—it's not worth the effort, think again! When done well, delegation leads to:

1. **Increased capacity.** By offloading tasks to your team, you free up time to focus on higher-level priorities.

2. **Team development.** Delegation provides opportunities for your team members to grow, learn new skills, and take on more responsibility.

3. **Better outcomes.** When team members are empowered to own tasks, they bring fresh perspectives and ideas that can lead to improved results.

But how do you get delegation right? This is where the **Pause-Consider-Act** framework comes into play.

Step 1: Pause

Before jumping into a task or project yourself, take a moment to **Pause**. Managers often feel the urge to jump in and get things done themselves, especially when they know the task well or can handle it quickly. But pausing allows you to step back and evaluate whether this is something you should do or whether it's an opportunity to delegate.

Ask yourself, *Is this task something only I can do?* And if the answer is yes, change the question to ask, *Is this task something only I should be doing?* More often than not, the answer is no. Even if you can do it faster or better, that doesn't mean you should. Your time as a manager is best spent on strategy, leadership, and guiding your team, not doing tasks that could be handled by someone else.

John, for example, could have paused and asked himself why he continued to do the reports. Was it really because no one else could handle them, or was it because he was clinging to a task that he believed was a key part of his identity? By taking that pause, John could have seen the bigger picture and recognized that being known as a great manager (and delegator) was a lot more impactful than being the "report guy," and letting go of the reports would not only free up his time but also give someone else the chance to grow.

Step 2: Consider

Once you've paused, it's time to **Consider** your options. Think about your team and their abilities. Who's ready to take on more responsibility? Who has the skills needed for this task? But don't stop there—also consider their current workload. Just because someone has the ability doesn't mean they have the capacity (or interest).

This is where many managers, like John, run into trouble. John eventually delegated the reports to his team member, Jane, but had a hard time fully letting go. He micromanaged every detail, frustrated that her bullet points didn't match his preferred style. To complicate things further, he had asked her to submit the reports by 5:00 P.M. on Thursdays, but one week, she sent them at 5:13. Feeling annoyed, John decided to take back a more hands-on role in overseeing the reports.

What he didn't realize was that Jane wasn't aware the bullet points were an issue or that they even mattered. She also didn't realize that her slightly late submission had caused such frustration, especially because she had already been starting her Thursdays two hours early just to fit the reports into her already full schedule. If John had paused to consider Jane's workload, clearly communicated his expectations, and reconsidered whether the style of bullet points really mattered to anyone but him, he could have empowered her to take ownership of the reports instead of making her feel micromanaged and reprimanded.

When deciding whom to delegate tasks to, also consider your team members' development goals. What skills are they looking to build? What areas could they grow in? Delegation isn't just about lightening your own workload; it's also a chance to help your team learn and stretch their abilities. Rotating tasks can be valuable for the team as a whole, but it's also important to delegate strategically.

For instance, if some team members are interested in pursuing management roles, give them leadership opportunities, like mentoring a colleague. For those who've expressed the opposite ("I like doing the job, but I don't want to manage anyone"), offer chances to share their expertise in other ways, such as creating a guide or leading a training session. This tailored approach ensures that delegation supports both team development and individual goals.

Step 3: Act

Finally, it's time to **Act**. But delegation isn't simply about handing off a task and walking away. To delegate effectively, you need to communicate clearly and set the person up for success.

Here's how:

- **Be specific** about what needs to be done and what the expectations are. What does success look like? What's the deadline? Who else might be involved?

- **Ask for their understanding** about what's expected. Don't assume that they know everything that's expected. Ask them to put it into their words, so you can make sure you were clear and didn't say anything wrong.

- **Ask for their plan** of how they'll realistically get it done. Don't assume they know how to juggle this new responsibility with their existing workload. Ask how they plan to balance it and offer to help reprioritize tasks if needed.

- **Provide support**, but don't hover. Checking in occasionally is important, but give your team member the space to take ownership of the task.

MANAGING UP AND ACROSS

Delegation doesn't stop with your team—it often involves managing relationships with peers and senior leaders as well. When you delegate tasks that involve cross-functional teams or other departments, it's important to loop in those leaders. They may expect perfection from your team, especially if they're used to working with you directly. Managing their expectations is key.

For instance, imagine you're delegating an important project to a team member who will collaborate with another department. It's likely that the other department's leadership is accustomed to working with you and may expect things to go perfectly. This is where managing across comes in. Let those leaders know your team member is stepping up and that this is an opportunity for them to learn and grow. If they have feedback or concerns, encourage them to share those with you first. This way, you can filter the feedback and help guide your team members constructively rather than overwhelming them with criticism.

Managing up is also critical when delegating. Senior leaders need to understand why you're delegating tasks and how it benefits the team. They may also need reminders about the day-to-day realities your team members face, especially as they take on more complex, higher-level work. Gaining their support is key because if they see delegation as merely offloading work, they might be less inclined to back you. However, when they understand that delegation is about building your team's capacity and developing future leaders, they'll be much more likely to support and champion the process.

One way to phrase it is, "You might remember what it felt like when you first tried something new, especially knowing that leaders at work would see it. We've been talking to our team members about their goals and providing them opportunities toward them. We want our team members to feel comfortable trying things out. I'm here to support them, give them room to take the lead, and provide feedback to help them keep improving along the way, and I appreciate your support by encouraging them as well." Communication is key. Keep them in the loop about the progress your team is making and highlight the growth you're seeing as a result of that delegation.

DELEGATION IN PRACTICE: REAL-WORLD EXAMPLES

Now, let's see how this framework plays out in three very different environments. How can delegation work in practice?

Example 1: Call Center Manager Delegating Quality Control

Lisa, a call center manager, has been handling quality control herself for years, and it's a task that eats up a lot of time. Her top employee, Sam, has been doing great work and mentioned more than once that he'd be interested in a corporate quality control position someday. Seeing an opportunity to help him take a step toward that goal, Lisa decides it could be time to pass the reviews over to him.

Before jumping in, Lisa takes a step back to think it through. Sure, Sam is good at what he does so he should be up to taking this on, but this is new territory for him, and she wants to make sure he has the space to do it well. She considers his workload and sets up a conversation to talk it over. During their chat, she explains why this task matters, describes what good results look like, and asks how he feels about adding it to his plate.

Sam's response is honest—he's been so efficient with his current work that he not only has extra capacity but has also been feeling a little bored lately. He's excited for the chance to take on something new and challenging. He reassures Lisa that he's not just saying what she wants to hear—he genuinely has the time and is ready to take this on. They agree on clear expectations: Sam will take an hour of his workday away from regular calls, dedicating that time to quality control instead. Sam promises to alert Lisa if he feels stretched too thin, while Lisa schedules training sessions and extra check-ins to make sure he feels supported as he takes on the new responsibility.

By pausing, considering, and acting, Lisa successfully delegates the task while giving Sam the chance to grow in his role.

Example 2: Retail District Manager
Delegating Store Operations

David, a district manager overseeing multiple retail stores, has always taken full responsibility for inventory management across his region. It's a high-stakes task that involves analyzing trends, identifying supply issues, and ensuring stores have the right products in stock. While David is confident in his process, he's been looking for ways to build his team's skills and prepare them for higher-level roles.

One of his top employees, Maria, has consistently impressed him with her initiative and reliability. Maria has also expressed interest in learning more about operations management, with a long-term goal of advancing to a regional role. Seeing an opportunity to help her grow, David decides to delegate part of the district's inventory management responsibilities to her.

So, he stops by the store and leaves Maria a note over the weekend, letting her know she'll be taking the process over for several locations and to reach out with any questions. But when she reads it Monday morning, she's not excited—she's frustrated. She immediately texts her former co-worker, "Good thing you got out. I'm getting more work dumped on me, no heads-up. Now I've got to travel, and I don't even know if I can expense gas."*

Why wouldn't Maria be excited, especially if she wants to grow? Because while David paused enough to think about development opportunities, he skipped the rest. He didn't consider Maria's current workload, the impact of adding travel, or explain specifically how reports were to be done. Most importantly, he didn't act, which would have meant having a conversation before making the decision.**

But they eventually did have a conversation. Because, fortunately, Maria didn't just vent to her former co-worker—she spoke up. When David visited the store later that week, she shared her concerns, and that's when he realized how this should've gone from the start. He took a step back and made a plan to do it the right way.

---

* As a manager, whether you're delegating or handling anything else, part of your role is considering the personal factors that matter to your team, especially when it comes to their time and money. Things like, "Can I expense this?" may seem small, but giving clear answers up front—and explaining how the process works—is a big help, especially for team members doing it for the first time.

** As we learned from Carrie Bradshaw, communicating critical information solely in writing isn't generally well received. (*Sex and the City*, Season 6, Episode 7, "The Post-It Always Sticks Twice," originally aired August 3, 2003.)

This time, David paused to really consider Maria's workload. She was already managing one of the busiest stores in the district, and now he was asking her to take on more responsibility across multiple locations. So, instead of pushing everything onto her, he decided to start small, offering a clear, manageable piece of the project: leading the audit process for her own store.

David mapped out how to help Maria succeed, including training on the reports, adding it to the agenda for their check-ins, and clearly answering her questions on things like travel expectations and reimbursements. When he sat down with Maria to walk through these, he also explained the opportunity, how it aligned with her career goals, and why it mattered to the district.

Maria appreciated that David took the time to hear her concerns and was willing to revisit his initial plan.* With the full picture— and a voice in the process—she felt more prepared and confident stepping up. Together, they worked through expectations and came up with a plan to help Maria delegate more responsibilities at her own store, so she could gradually take on inventory management for additional locations over time.

Maria also followed David's lead—his second approach, not the "please do this, thanks" note he left the first time. She used the same structure from their conversation—why the task mattered, what to do, and what support looked like—to delegate day-to-day responsibilities to her team. That freed up her time and energy to focus on her new role, without feeling overwhelmed.

David learned this lesson the hard way, when he could tell Maria wasn't happy. But he learned that good delegation and growth start with a conversation and a plan.

Example 3: Health Care Executive Delegating Training Facilitation Role

Julie is a health care executive at a hospital. One of her nurses, Alex, has expressed an interest in moving into hospital administration. Recognizing Alex's potential and his passion for learning, Julie

---

* It's great to be open to adjusting a plan. But asking for feedback *before* the plan is set often leads to even better results.

decides to delegate part of an upcoming training session to him, giving him an opportunity to gain hands-on experience with the administrative side of the hospital.

Before making any decisions, Julie schedules a one-on-one meeting with Alex to gauge his interest. She explains the opportunity, outlining why she believes he's well suited for it and what it would involve. Julie emphasizes that this is a chance for Alex to gain experience and grow professionally, but also reassures him that it's not something he's expected to take on if the timing doesn't feel right.

Alex is enthusiastic about the opportunity and shares that he's been looking for ways to develop his skills beyond his clinical role. He admits he's concerned about balancing the project with his nursing responsibilities, so Julie assures him they'll work together to adjust his workload and ensure he has time to focus on the training without feeling overwhelmed.

As promised, Julie reaches out to the nurse scheduling team to discuss adjusting Alex's hours. She explains the importance of the project and Alex's role in it, ensuring that his clinical responsibilities are covered during the times he's preparing for the training. Together, they develop a plan to reduce Alex's clinical shifts a bit for the duration of the project, redistributing coverage among the team.

Julie then meets with Alex to share the updated plan. She explains how his schedule will shift to provide protected time for the project while also making sure that patient care won't be disrupted. Alex is relieved and excited, knowing he can have time to prepare without sacrificing the quality of his work with patients.

Alex's responsibilities include reviewing the existing training materials, identifying areas for improvement, and incorporating updates to make the content more engaging and practical. Julie encourages him to meet with employees who have previously completed the training, asking for honest feedback on what worked well and what could be improved. She also stresses the importance of acknowledging contributions and giving credit to those who took the time to provide their input.

Julie's calendar included time blocked out to consider her team members and what they were working on.* As she reflected on Alex's upcoming session, she felt good about his preparation and how he'd been communicating. But just to be sure, she typed an AI prompt: *"What else should I do to help my nurse's first training session go well?"*

The response made her pause. One of the suggestions was, *"Consider whether any proactive communication to attendees could help set the training up for success."* That's when she realized she'd almost missed a critical step, because that suggestion brought up a lesson from the past. She once sat through a training where someone was leading a session for the first time. On paper, they were ready—the material was solid—but they weren't prepared for that audience. The group? Experienced medical professionals who expected perfection. The questions started flying right away, including, "Is this training why I didn't get a response to my patient question yesterday?" You could see it rattled the trainer. She made it through, but Julie never saw her volunteer to lead a session again.

Julie didn't want that to happen to Alex.

So this time she made sure to set the stage. She communicated Alex's upcoming session to the other hospital administrators and department leaders, explaining why this was a great growth opportunity for him. She highlighted the benefit of having someone with clinical experience running the training and let them know his schedule had been adjusted so he could focus on getting ready. Julie also asked the leadership team to support Alex if and when he reached out to other colleagues for their input, and she told them to bring any concerns or feedback about the session directly to her, so she could coach him through it.

On the day of the training, Alex not only delivered his updated section, but he also followed Julie's advice by sharing how the changes were shaped by the feedback he received, calling out specific colleagues by name and giving them credit for their ideas. The group asked questions, but it didn't feel like an inquisition.

---

* Quick tip: Add this to your calendar. A few minutes of intentional thinking time goes a long way in supporting your team, but it's easy to forget without a reminder. You can call it whatever you want—maybe "Team Development" or "1:1 Prep"—just make sure you'll know what it means later. A code name like "Project Q" might sound perfect now, but when it pops up next week, you'll probably have no idea what it's for.

The conversation stayed constructive, and the feedback made the training even stronger.

The training was a success for a few reasons. Colleagues appreciated hearing Alex recognize their input. They hadn't expected him to do that publicly, but they appreciated it. It made them look good to their own managers. The leaders in the room noticed, too—both how prepared Alex was and the way Julie had clearly put thought into how she delegated the session. One of them even pulled Julie aside afterward and asked, "Mind if I steal this for my team? And do you have a cheat sheet I could use?"

And the best part? Alex really enjoyed it. He told Julie he'd been interested in moving into administration but was nervous about how this would go. Now, he wanted to keep building on it and lead more trainings.

For Julie, having a few extra conversations with Alex, and other leaders, to prep for the session took more time than just saying, "Go lead the training." But it was still far less time—and far more effective—than if she'd just done it herself.

DELEGATION CHECKLIST FOR MANAGERS

If you'd like a "success sheet"* to ensure you're delegating effectively, use this checklist as a guide:

1. **Pause.** Before taking on a task, ask yourself, *Is this something I need to do myself?*

2. **Consider.** Who on your team has the skills and capacity to take this on? How does this fit into their development goals?

3. **Set clear expectations.** Outline the task, define success, and communicate any deadlines or key milestones.

---

* A term I like to use instead of "cheat sheet."

4. **Provide support.** Ask for their plan and offer to help them balance their workload if needed. Be available for questions without hovering.

5. **Manage across.** Inform other leaders who will be involved and manage their expectations. Encourage them to share feedback with you so you can guide your team members.

6. **Recognize effort.** Acknowledge the work your team member has put in and celebrate their successes, even if there are areas for improvement.

7. **Ask yourself, *What am I missing?* When delegating, try using an AI prompt like: *"What should I keep in mind when delegating a project about [general topic] to a team member who [insert general details, like is new to the team or is looking to grow into a new role]?"* It's a simple way to catch things you might overlook.

Delegation is more than just getting things off your to-do list; it's about fostering growth for both your team and yourself. By using the **Pause-Consider-Act** framework, you can delegate with intention, set your team members up for success, and manage relationships across the organization. Regardless of your team's workplace setting, thoughtful delegation is a powerful way to develop a stronger, more capable team while reducing your own stress.

Questions for Self-Reflection

- **What holds me back from delegating more tasks?**

  Consider whether it's a fear of losing control, worrying the task won't be done right, or even concern about not being seen as valuable. Identifying the root of the hesitation is the first step toward addressing it.

- **How might addressing this hesitation benefit both me and my team?**

  Imagine how much time you'd free up for bigger priorities by delegating more, and at the same time, you'd be giving your team the chance to grow, take on new challenges, and feel trusted in their roles.

- **When was the last time I delegated a task, and how did it affect my workload and my team's development?**

  Reflect on whether the delegation was successful and what you might do differently next time.

- **Are there tasks I'm currently holding on to that someone else on my team could handle?**

  Think about whether you're keeping certain tasks out of habit or control and how delegating them could benefit both you and your team.

- **How do I ensure my team members have the capacity and support needed when I delegate?**

  Consider how you balance workloads, provide guidance, and manage expectations with other leaders when delegating responsibilities.

Chapter 7

Accountability Without Micromanagement

I'll never forget the moment at work when I was handed a massive project with the expectation to complete it in just one month. It wasn't an "ask" as much as it was "You're going to own this now." Without skipping a beat, I said, "Of course. I'll take care of it." No hesitation, no pushback, no questions. But the reality? I already had more than a full plate of work. Even if I worked 24/7, there was literally no way to get it done. Still, I didn't pause to think, or say to my boss, "I can't realistically do this, or ask the one critical question: How am I actually going to do this?"

Instead of putting together an actual plan, I leaned hard into wishful thinking. I kept telling myself that the usual chaos would calm down and somehow, I'd find extra time to focus. Spoiler: It didn't calm down, and I didn't find any extra time. The urgent to-dos kept coming, and I spent every day doing the same things I always did, because I didn't have space for anything else. It wasn't a strategy; it was just hoping for a break that never came.

Suddenly, it was near the end of the month and I had barely touched the project. I'd wake up in the middle of the night with a pit in my stomach. The deadline was staring me down, and panic set in. Adrenaline kicked in right behind it. I scrambled, racing to finish, fueled more by stress than strategy. Somehow, I got it done.

But this isn't a feel-good story. Because the work? It *wasn't* good. Honestly, it was one of the worst things I've ever turned in. And I wasn't any better myself. I was completely wiped out—physically, mentally, emotionally. Even days later, I was still drained, still frustrated, and wondering how I let it get that far—and how to make sure I never ended up there again.

Looking back, the mistake wasn't just that I said yes; it was that I didn't stop to figure out how I was actually going to deliver. I didn't take a realistic look at what was already on my plate, and I definitely didn't raise my hand to say, "I'm maxed out." But here's the thing—it shouldn't fall entirely on employees to do that. Managers who understand people will prioritize checking in on workload and creating a culture where it's not just okay to ask for help—it's expected. Without that kind of support, it's easy for things to fall through the cracks. That project may have slipped, but what it really revealed was a deeper issue: accountability—on both sides.

ACCOUNTABILITY: NOT ABOUT BLAME, BUT SUPPORT

The term *accountability* often gets a bad reputation. People hear it and immediately think of blame or punishment. But accountability can be a *good* thing by creating a system of support, making sure you and your team are on the right track, and delivering what's needed without sacrificing well-being. It's not just about getting things done; it's about *how* they get done and making sure everyone has what they need to succeed.

In the previous chapter, we talked about how the **Pause-Consider-Act** framework helps with delegation. Now, let's apply it to accountability. As a manager, it's critical you and your team take time to reflect before jumping into any new task. Any "yes" shouldn't be just a superficial "Yes, I'll do it" (because they're afraid of disappointing you); it should come after really pausing to assess how it fits in with everything else. Consider what resources are available and what other priorities are in play, and then act thoughtfully with a clear plan.

Step 1: Pause: Teaching Your Team What Really Matters

Before jumping into any task, it's important to remember the first step, **Pause**, and ground everything in what really matters—the larger organizational goals. Earlier in this book, we discussed setting clear expectations with your team about the company's mission and their role in achieving it. If you haven't done that yet, now's a great time to start.

Imagine your organization's focus is "exceptional customer service." It's a great message for a commercial or an employee handbook, but how does it translate into daily actions? How do team members deliver on that promise when they're having a tough day? What should they prioritize when faced with competing demands? And what happens if they're depending on colleagues who don't follow through? These are the kinds of questions your team needs you to address so they can confidently approach their work, ensuring their actions align with the organization's larger goals.

When holding your team members accountable, it's essential to frame it with the "why." Whether they're working with external clients or internal colleagues, help them see how their individual contributions affect the larger team or business outcomes. For example, if a team member is responsible for getting reports to another department, making or missing that deadline doesn't just impact them; it also has a ripple effect across the entire workflow.

This clarity can also help them understand that when they say yes to a new project, it's not just about adding another task to their to-do list. It's about really making sure they're thinking about how that task fits into the broader organizational goals and finding ways to ensure it gets done without letting other priorities drop or suffer in quality.

Step 2: Consider: Balancing Workload and Setting Realistic Expectations

The **Consider** step is where you, as the manager, help your team balance their workload. It's not enough for your team member to say, "Yes, I can do that." You need to make sure that they can answer the question "How are you going to do it?"—and that starts with you asking them.

We all have days when things feel like too much, when our personal lives or even professional hurdles make it hard to show up the same way we did yesterday or in the way we'll be able to tomorrow. So, how do you help your team manage those times? Encourage them to think about how they can meet deadlines while maintaining balance, ensuring the quality of their work and their life outside of work don't take a hit. Sometimes, longer hours may be required (and hopefully, you made that clear in the interview process, as we discussed earlier!). But if they can't do it all, what can they reprioritize or delegate? Encourage them to be honest about what's possible and create an environment where it's okay to raise a hand and say, "I need help."

By considering the challenges your team members face and working with them to prioritize their workload, you're not just holding them accountable for deadlines—you're also teaching them how to manage their time and energy effectively.

Step 3: Act: Clear Communication and Regular Check-Ins

The final step is to **Act**. This isn't just about assigning a task and walking away. It's about setting clear expectations, checking in regularly, and providing support. One of the best ways to make accountability a positive experience is by explaining it as a proactive process to keep everyone on track, rather than scrambling at the last minute to meet deadlines.

As I mentioned earlier, when you delegate tasks, explain the why behind them. Make sure your team members understand the big picture. If they're unsure of something, encourage them to ask questions early on. And as a manager, it's your job to check in *well before* the deadline. A quick mid-project check-in allows you to course-correct if needed and ensures no one feels overwhelmed or stuck when it's too late to adjust.

Most importantly, it's about setting clear, sustainable expectations. Everyone should walk away from a meeting or conversation about an assignment with clarity on exactly what they're responsible for, how to approach it, and when it's due. Provide specific details and realistic timelines, and then ask them to walk you through their plan. For example, if, on a Friday, you tell a team member that you need something "next week," and they respond, "I'll have it done by Monday morning," take a moment to clarify. Are they planning to work over the weekend to meet what they perceive as an urgent deadline (and is it really urgent)? Or do they feel pressure to prioritize it because their upcoming week is already packed? Use this conversation to check in on their workload, and consider how adding weekend work might affect their personal plans and long-term energy and engagement. Clear communication and accountability aren't just about getting things done—they're about ensuring your team can deliver their best work long term without adding unnecessary stress.

BUILDING ACCOUNTABILITY INTO TEAM CULTURE

Accountability becomes a powerful tool when it's a positive part of your team's culture, not just a scary word brought up when things go wrong. To build this kind of culture, focus on creating an environment where accountability feels constructive and supportive. One way to do this is by using team meetings as a platform for open, honest conversations about workload, deadlines, and the resources needed for success.

Try this exercise in your next team meeting: Ask your team, "How do the way we meet deadlines and the effort we put into our work impact not only our success but also the experience of the people we work with?" This can open up a meaningful discussion about how each person's contributions impact not just the team but also the wider organization, and even your customers, patients, clients, guests, vendors, or other stakeholders who rely on the quality and reliability of your work.

Next, follow up with, "How do you show up when you're having a tough day? How do you communicate if you're struggling, whether it's meeting a deadline or just not feeling your best? And how does it help when others are up front about their challenges, instead of it coming through in missed deadlines or minimal effort?" It's important for team members to know that it's okay to be human and ask for help. Encourage them to share strategies for managing tough days and to feel comfortable approaching you or their colleagues if they need support. Normalizing these conversations not only creates a supportive environment but also reinforces the importance of accountability. When team members understand how their actions—or inactions—impact others, it creates a sense of shared responsibility that strengthens the entire team.

Help your team see accountability as being the kind of colleague they'd want to work with. It goes beyond simply meeting expectations; it's also about supporting each other in maintaining a healthy balance between work and life. Remind them that holding one another accountable isn't about pointing fingers; it's about staying aligned and working together toward shared goals. This kind of accountability is strongest when everyone communicates openly, checks in regularly, and offers support throughout the process.

DISCUSS WORK-LIFE BALANCE AND DEADLINE MANAGEMENT

How can you support your team in meeting deadlines without unduly sacrificing personal time or burning out? Again, start by asking your team, "How do you balance meeting deadlines with your other work responsibilities and your life outside of work?" This question takes trust and opens the door to a discussion about how they approach their workload and manage their time.

Talk through strategies for time management, prioritization, and setting realistic goals. Share your own thoughts and tips, but also encourage the team to share what works for them. This not only helps everyone learn from each other but also reinforces the idea that meeting deadlines is a shared responsibility, not just something they have to figure out on their own.

It's also important to create a space where team members feel comfortable admitting when they're struggling. Say something like, "If things ever start to feel overwhelming, how can we talk about it together?" This lets your team know it's okay to bring up challenges before they escalate. By having these conversations, you're building a culture where accountability doesn't mean overextending to the point of burnout; it means finding sustainable ways to stay productive and motivated.

Remember, you're not just managing a team for today; you're also shaping how they grow and succeed throughout their careers. When your team feels supported and able to manage their workload in a sustainable way, they're more likely to meet deadlines, stay engaged, and remain motivated for the long term. That's what accountability is all about: working together to deliver results you're counting on now, while maintaining the energy and drive to keep showing up and performing at their best long term.

BUILDING ACCOUNTABILITY IN YOUR TEAM MEETINGS: WHAT TO KEEP IN MIND

Here are themes and questions you can use in your next team meeting to build a culture of accountability:

1. **Accountability as a positive.** Frame accountability as a process that ensures quality work, makes us reliable colleagues, and allows us to maintain a healthy work-life balance.

2. **Anchor in goals.** Start by asking, "What are our organizational goals, and how do we each contribute to them?" Highlight how individual accountability connects to the bigger picture and reinforces the impact of each team member's work.

3. **Show up for others.** Discuss with your team, "How does it matter how we show up for others?" and "What strategies can we use when we're having a tough day?" These questions encourage reflection on accountability and teamwork, so showing up and supporting one another become second nature.

4. **Honest conversations about workload.** Ask, "How do we balance deadlines without sacrificing our personal lives? If it's too much, how can we talk about it?" Encourage them to speak up before things feel overwhelming.

5. **Clear expectations.** Emphasize that each team member should always clearly understand what's expected of them, why it matters, and when it's due. Regular check-ins should be a routine part of your team's process, not just something that happens when problems arise. Make it clear that if something outside their control is causing a roadblock—like waiting on someone else—they need to let you know. You can't address an issue you're unaware of, and it's far better to tackle the problem together than to risk it looking like you're passing blame on to someone else when explaining delays to a senior leader.

Accountability, when approached with the **Pause-Consider-Act** framework, can transform how your team works together. It's not about blaming or micromanaging; it's about teaching your team to take ownership of their work while feeling supported. By creating a space where everyone clearly understands how their work fits into the larger picture, open communication is the norm, and your team feels comfortable asking for help, you're setting them up for long-term success. Accountability isn't about pushing from behind or chasing someone far ahead; it's about walking alongside your team, offering guidance, and ensuring everyone stays on track. *That* kind of accountability is what gets results and grows careers—yours included.

Questions for Self-Reflection

- **Does "accountability" have a negative connotation for me or my team?**

  Think about how you and your team view accountability. Is it associated with blame, or is it seen as a positive way to ensure success?

- **How can I make accountability feel more collaborative and supportive?**

  Reflect on ways you can shift the narrative around accountability to one that focuses on teamwork and shared goals, rather than on mistakes.

- **How can I share ideas and tips to be more efficient and productive while making sure everyone gets credit for their contributions (as a team and an organization)?**

  Building a culture of idea-sharing starts with focusing on collaboration, not criticism. Take a moment to reflect on how you can recognize and reward people for helping each other, and how your team and organization could do it more broadly.

- **How can I naturally incorporate conversations about workload and support into my one-on-one meetings, making them more conversational and productive?**

  Think about how to create an open, conversational environment where your team feels comfortable sharing challenges before they become overwhelming. Sometimes the roadblocks they face are real—like a process bottleneck or lack of resources—and other times it might come down to their effort. How can you tell the difference? Start by listening, asking thoughtful questions, and digging into what's behind the challenge. Understanding whether it's a genuine issue or a matter of accountability helps you respond in a way that's fair, realistic, and supportive.

- **How can I hold myself accountable to discuss potential challenges and anticipate issues before they arise?**

  Think about having regular, proactive conversations with your team (in group meetings or one-on-ones), including asking about past experiences or potential scenarios that could cause delays. Discuss what's happened before, what could go wrong, and how you can work together to either avoid or respond to those roadblocks, making it easier to manage the unexpected.

Chapter 8

Balancing Work and Life (Without Losing Your Mind)

When I think about taking time off work, there's one trip I'll never forget. It was a beach trip with friends—planned months in advance and marked with big stars on my calendar. We had nonstop text threads debating which house to rent, who'd be on cooking duty, and whether we needed three matching dinner outfits or five. It was the kind of trip that promised laughter, late-night talks, and (finally) a real break from everything. But as the departure date crept closer, my excitement started to fade. The fun wasn't the issue—if anything, it kept sounding better and better. What weighed on me was everything I'd need to finish at work before I could actually walk out the door. The deadlines, the half-done projects, the last-minute e-mails—it all started to pile up until I found myself wondering whether I could even enjoy the trip at all. Was this time off really going to feel like a break . . . or just another source of stress?

I kept telling myself it would all feel better once I got there and could finally relax. But when the trip did arrive, the stress came with me. Last-minute emergencies popped up before I left, so I packed my laptop, convincing myself I'd just open it for a few minutes each morning and still enjoy the rest of the day. But then new "quick questions" came up, and I couldn't shut it down—or so I felt. I spent all day working while my friends were out enjoying the beach. They gently joked about me missing the fun, and I played them off. But inside, I wanted to cry. I felt trapped. I was trying to balance the expectation to work with my hope (and need) to finally relax, and in the end, I didn't do either. I wasn't present with my friends, and I didn't feel like I was doing enough work, either.

By the time the trip was over, I was more drained than when it started. Honestly, I was angry and filled with regret—regret for taking the trip, for working so hard, and for not being able to actually take a vacation. The relaxation I'd been counting on was nowhere to be found, and all the stress I tried to escape was there the whole time. I missed out on precious time and memories with the people I care about because I couldn't fully step away from work.

If any of that hits home, I'm really sorry—it's tough. That mix of guilt, pressure to stay connected, and wondering whether stepping away is even worth it is something a lot of people wrestle with. And if you're a manager, that weight often feels even heavier. But here's the thing: That's exactly why taking time off matters. It's not just about rest—it's about making this job, this career, and this life sustainable. That's what this chapter is here for: to help make time off more realistic, less stressful, and something you can actually enjoy.

THE REALITY OF TIME OFF FOR MANAGERS: WHY IT FEELS IMPOSSIBLE

I openly talk with others about this struggle and frequently hear, "It's just not possible to actually disconnect as a manager." Why? I hear lots of reasons:

- "If I'm not around, things will fall apart."
- "No one can do it as easily as I can."
- "It will take longer to show someone else than it will to do it myself."
- "My team's already busy, and I don't want to add to their stress."

- "Taking time off will only make things worse because I'll come back to a pile of work I can't handle."

- "If my team can get everything done when I'm not there, then it will look like I'm not needed. And that's not a good thing—that's a one-way ticket to getting laid off."

Do any (or all) of these sound familiar? You may remember some of these from Chapter 6, because challenges at work often bleed into other areas. If you haven't trained anyone else to do what you're doing, then you have to be the one to do it or it won't get done. So, you either don't take time off or take it off, but make it a "working vacation." And when the emphasis is on "working" rather than "vacation," it turns a much-needed break into an unintended source of stress.

Taking time off to recharge comes with significant benefits—not just for you, but also for your team. Research shows that managers who take breaks have an improved mood, think more clearly, and have a boost in creativity.[1] On the flip side, failing to step away and recharge can lead to serious consequences, including higher levels of stress, burnout, and declining performance. Managers who don't prioritize rest face greater anxiety and mental fatigue, which can have long-term negative effects on both your well-being and your ability to lead effectively. In other words, the time you take off next week could shape the success of your career far longer.

For a real-life example of how a vacation can spark ideas that lead to unexpected career breakthroughs, look outside the traditional workplace, to Broadway—specifically, Lin-Manuel Miranda. After dedicating seven years to bringing his first major project—the musical *In the Heights*, to the stage, Miranda finally allowed himself a much-deserved vacation. During the long-overdue beach trip, he picked up Ron Chernow's biography of Alexander Hamilton. As he read, inspiration struck: Hamilton's life would make an incredible musical. Reflecting on that moment, Miranda said, "The moment my brain got a moment's rest, Hamilton walked into it."[2]

This groundbreaking idea, which went on to redefine Broadway, only came to him because he allowed himself the space to step back and recharge.

Time off isn't just a luxury or something to squeeze in when you can—it's a necessity to become and stay sharp, productive, and creative in your role. Without taking breaks to recharge, you risk running on empty, and eventually, it will catch up to you. And here's the challenge: When you look back at your career, what do you want to remember? The long hours you put in, the late-night e-mails, and the extra hours and days sacrificed for work? Or will you think about the memories of time spent with family, vacations that helped you reset, and the experiences that made life fulfilling? How can you actually prioritize and make the most of those experiences, now?

Because "now" matters—it's not just about endlessly promising yourself you'll take time off "someday." It's easy to fall into the trap of thinking that continuously working and "grinding" guarantees greater success, but in reality, the opposite is often true. The best leaders understand the importance of stepping back, recharging, and returning with fresh energy and ideas. Sustained strong performance comes from balance, not burnout. Consider the example you want to set for your team: Do you want to be thought of as someone who's constantly frazzled and exhausted, or as a leader who models healthy boundaries and inspires others to find balance?

Effectively taking time off is a leadership strategy. When your team sees you constantly working, whether it's during vacations, late at night, or never taking a break, it sets an unspoken expectation that they need to do the same. This can create a high-pressure environment where team members feel like they can't step away or disconnect, even when they *really* need, and deserve, to. Over time, this leads to disengagement, decreased productivity, and even burnout as the stress builds across the team.

The impact goes beyond daily stress and has long-term consequences. Consider succession planning. You may have team members who you know have incredible leadership potential. You may even have formal development plans or a succession planning organizational chart for those ready to step in when there's an opening. But will they want it? The answer to that question matters. If your team sees that being in a leadership role means constantly sacrificing time and energy, they might decide it's not worth it. For example, if they hear stories about leaders spending their entire vacation glued to calls or catching up on e-mails, or even see them responding constantly while "out of office," it sends a clear message: Stepping into leadership means giving up work-life balance. That can make people think twice about stepping into leadership, eventually leaving a gap in the pipeline, not because they're not ready for leadership, but because they just don't want it.

A culture of overwork impacts more than just one person or one vacation. It can threaten the sustainability of your team and the entire organization. Succession planning becomes more difficult when roles are seen as excessively demanding. If potential leaders opt out because of the examples set by current leadership, the organization risks facing leadership gaps during transitions. Normalizing the importance of truly recharging isn't just about giving your teams a chance for a great vacation*—it's also about protecting the organization's long-term leadership and success.

BURNOUT: THE RIPPLE IMPACTS

You might think, *Yes, I know I work too much and don't take vacation enough, but I'm working on taking steps (like reading this book!), and I always tell my team that they don't need to work the way I do.* That's a great start—recognizing and setting those expectations is important. But actions truly do speak louder than words. Whether you explicitly expect your team to be constantly working or you're just leading by example, your behavior sets the tone. No matter what you say, if you're always on, they'll feel the pressure to do the same. It's easy for them to start by following your example and spiral into working nonstop to try to get ahead, which can take a toll on their relationships and health, resulting in burnout.

---

* However, this is incredibly important and will likely be appreciated by your team members and their families and friends even more than you might realize.

When burnout is caused by work stress, it often strikes at the worst possible time—right in the middle of a major project, when the team is already stretched thin, or you're launching a new product. And then, just when you're counting on them most, that team member comes to you and says they've hit their limit—they can't do it anymore. They're leaving. Suddenly, your panic sets in. You think, *What's going to happen to the project? How will team members react—will they leave, too? Can I afford to lose this person right now?* It's a stark reminder that while the work matters, everything ultimately depends on the well-being of your team.

In moments like these, you realize the true cost of excessive stress. It doesn't just impact that one person—it can throw your entire operation into chaos. That's why setting an example by balancing your own workload and taking time off is crucial. When your team sees you not just *talking* about taking time off but actually *taking* it (and being off, not "off-ish" by spending hours checking in on them each day), they can feel more empowered to do the same, which ultimately can get—and keep—everyone performing at their best.

Your leadership is more than just making sure work gets done day-to-day. You're impacting your team members—how they do their job, how they perform in their careers, and how they live outside of work. And doing that well is true leadership. If your team sees you prioritizing your own well-being and taking breaks, they'll recognize that leadership doesn't have to come at the cost of personal health. By modeling healthy behavior, you're showing them that success in leadership is about balance, not constant availability.

Think of a team member (or someone you know) who would make an incredible leader. Picture the exact moment you offer them a promotion—the pride you feel, and the excitement you're sure they will. Now imagine the difference between two scenarios: In one, they avoid eye contact as they turn it down, saying, "I want to be able to actually watch my kids grow up." That stings. But in the other, they eagerly accept without hesitation because they've seen your example—a leader who grows in their career and takes on responsibility without constantly apologizing to family or losing friendships.

Future leaders need to see that it's possible to find real success while still living a real life. If "success" always seems to come with an impressive title but never the freedom to enjoy a Friday night without conference calls, they might decide to step off the corporate ladder altogether. But when they see you prioritizing self-care while leading effectively, they'll feel confident stepping into those roles when the time comes.

Giving Your Team Opportunities to Grow

Taking time off isn't just about your well-being; it's also about creating opportunities for your team to grow. When you step away, your team gets the chance to take on new responsibilities, make decisions, and build their confidence, ultimately strengthening the whole team. Like delegation, it's natural to feel uneasy about handing things off, especially if it's because you'll be away. You might worry the work won't meet your standards (or preferences), or that things could go wrong. But it's important to reframe this: It's not about you—it's about giving your team the space to step up and shine.

By allowing your team to handle responsibilities in your absence, you're not only helping them develop their skills but also showing you trust them. This boosts their confidence and, over time, creates a stronger, more capable team. The more you empower your team to take ownership, the more effective they'll become.

Revisiting Delegation: Applying It When You're Off

Before you take time off, revisit those delegation strategies we discussed in Chapter 6. Effective delegation is more than just handing off tasks—it's about thoughtful planning, clear communication, and building trust within your team. When you're going to be away, these principles become even more important. They can be done with a very manageable amount of thoughtful planning.

One of the biggest mistakes managers make is waiting until the last minute (or until after they've already left) to delegate their responsibilities. It often happens in a moment of realization—*Oh shoot, I forgot to tell them I'm going to be out!* That last-minute panic sets in, leaving you scrambling to offload tasks and your team feeling ambushed and unprepared. This creates unnecessary pressure and leaves your team scrambling to cover everything. Instead, plan ahead. Start delegating key tasks and responsibilities several weeks before your time off. Put it on your calendar and talk about it with your team, to allow them plenty of time to adjust and ask questions. The more time you give them to really understand what's expected—rather than scrambling to figure it out from a voice mail you leave during the few minutes you get cell service on your trip—the smoother everything will run while you're away.

Remember, successful delegation isn't about ensuring every task is done exactly as you would do it. It's about trusting your team to handle things in their own way. Give them the space to take ownership, make decisions, and learn from the experience. While it may feel uncomfortable at first, this trust allows your team to grow and builds their confidence in managing challenges. Plus, when they know you trust them, they're more likely to take initiative and solve problems in your absence, rather than just doing the bare minimum to avoid issues. This makes your time off more productive for everyone. Preparing for time off in this way strengthens your team's ability to handle future challenges. Who would've thought that a vacation for you could double as a development opportunity for them?

THE PAUSE-CONSIDER-ACT FRAMEWORK: MAKING TIME FOR YOURSELF AND YOUR TEAM

If the thought of taking time off still feels challenging, that's okay. Making changes to how you may have worked for years rarely happens overnight (or in just a few pages). It's common for managers to struggle with stepping away. It's important to remember that taking time off is not just something you need, but something you deserve. And as with every choice as a manager, the **Pause-Consider-Act** framework can help you navigate taking time off with more clarity and intention. You can use it to help you begin (and keep) finding ways to step away while ensuring your team is well prepared during your absence.

Pause

Start by pausing to reflect on your previous experiences with time off. Have you ever truly disconnected, or were you constantly checking e-mails, stressing about what might go wrong, or feeling guilty for being away? Take a moment to acknowledge what it would be like to actually be off—if you could leave your laptop at home, not dial into that meeting, or have others left in charge that you can trust to make decisions.

And pause to remember that time off is essential—not just for your well-being but also for your effectiveness as a leader. If you don't recharge, you can't be at your best. Remind yourself that you deserve this time and that a well-prepared team can handle things without you for a while. This reflection lays the groundwork; acknowledging the importance of breaks and how often you've truly taken them increases the chances that you'll consider how to take action.

Consider

Now, consider what it takes to fully step away. Start by identifying who needs to know that you'll be off. Should you let leadership know about your time off ahead of time and ensure it's planned for a convenient period? (*Yes!*) How will you communicate with your team to ensure they feel prepared and confident in your absence? Beyond simply assigning tasks, consider what systems you can implement to support your team while you're away. What responsibilities can you delegate, and who's best suited to handle them? Are there team members who might need additional guidance or support to succeed? Planning ahead ensures your team can thrive even when you're not there.

It's important to think through the details of your time off: Will you have access to e-mail, or are you planning a full digital detox? For instance, maybe you leave the laptop at home and just use your phone. If an emergency arises, who else could step in for support? If truly needed, how should your team contact you? Will you share your personal phone number, and more importantly, how will you define an emergency that you need to know? You can ask an AI prompt like: *"What should I think about as a manager in [role] when planning my time off, so I can actually unplug but my team knows what to do while I'm out?"*

AI can be a great tool—but don't forget to involve your team in the process, too. Discuss these questions with your team ahead of time. Ask them directly, "What situations might come up while I'm away where you'd need my help? And what might you want my help with?" Their responses can help clarify expectations. Instead of saying, "Call me if anything comes up," you'll have a clear playbook, helping your team distinguish between urgent matters and things they can handle independently.

It's also important to consider how your team might feel about your time away. Because, yes, we've discussed how your team can appreciate seeing you actually taking time off. But also, some team members may be afraid of it. They may worry about being blamed if something goes wrong or feel unsure about how to make decisions in your absence. To address their concerns, talk about it. Encourage open communication before you leave by asking, "What situations make you nervous, and how can I help you feel more prepared?" Let them know you're not expecting perfection—you're expecting effort, thoughtfulness, and teamwork. Reassure them that mistakes are part of growth and that you trust their judgment. Don't forget to vocally add that your confidence in their abilities is why you trust them to handle things in your absence.

Act

Finally, it's time to act. Don't wait until the last minute to start preparing for your time off—take the time to create a playbook to record and delegate your responsibilities well in advance. Once you have it, you can update it so you can reduce the pressure when you're off. Begin by mapping out key tasks and explaining them to your team weeks ahead of your break. Then, use the playbook to outline who will take on specific roles and provide guidelines for decision-making and troubleshooting in your absence. Giving your team time to ask questions and gradually take ownership ensures they feel comfortable and confident handling things while you're away. Be clear in your communication—set expectations for how often (if at all) you'll be checking in, how they can think through decisions that need to be made without you, what constitutes an emergency, who they can reach out to for approval or advice, and how they can reach you if truly necessary. To make sure it actually helps your team, don't finish the playbook and send it off seconds before you go offline. Have your team review it in advance to see whether anything's unclear, or whether it brings up other questions or other topics to add. Your playbook will be their guide, so make sure it's as detailed as needed to empower them to act independently while understanding what's expected.

Once you shut down, then what? It's natural to feel the urge to check in, especially if you're used to staying connected. But work to resist that instinct. If you've told your team you'll be off and trust them to manage things, it's important to honor that—for you and for them. For yourself, if you've committed to taking time off but then get back into old habits, you'll likely feel the guilt creep up.

But for your team, if you're constantly checking in, even with good intentions, that undermines their confidence and sends a mixed message about your trust in their abilities. Your intention of, "I want to show them I'm always there for them" is more likely seen as "My manager can never take a vacation and doesn't trust me to handle things." Give yourself permission to truly disconnect, knowing that your team has the tools and instructions they need from the playbook you've prepared. Remind yourself that recharging is not only good for your well-being but also a form of professional development. If you doubt that, just listen to more wise words from Lin-Manual Miranda: "Because of phones, we always have the ability to jump out of ourselves. But unless you learn how to be in your head, you'll never learn how to create."[3] Also, remember that your team's real growth happens when they figure things out without you giving them step-by-step instructions. Sure, there will be hiccups, but the progress they gain and the relaxation you get will be worth it.

When you return from time off, it's important to reengage with intention and purpose. First, give yourself time to settle back in—block off time to catch up on e-mails, go over key updates, and ease back into the workflow without feeling rushed. Instead of immediately jumping back into every detail or project, frame your first meeting with the team as an open discussion. Ask thoughtful questions to get a sense of how things went in your absence: "What went smoothly while I was out? Were there any unexpected challenges? How did the team handle those situations? Is there anything we can improve on for next time?" These questions allow you to get a comprehensive update without making your team feel like you're micromanaging or second-guessing their decisions. This approach also shows that you trust them to handle things independently and are more interested in learning and improving together for the future.

CHECKING IN WITHOUT MICROMANAGING

I know I've said this more than once, but it's worth repeating: Your time off should actually feel like time off. You deserve to fully unplug and recharge—and yes, that's absolutely the goal. But that's often easier said than done, and it might take some time to shift into that mindset. Be honest with yourself about why you're checking in and consider what steps you can take to break that habit. If you're worried your team won't know what to do, think about what more you can put in place before you leave so they feel more confident. And if you're concerned about getting blamed if your team makes a bad decision, proactively remind other leaders and your own manager that your team is covering in your absence. Let them know you've prepared your team as much as possible, but they may need some grace and, eventually, constructive feedback.

If you still feel the need to stay somewhat connected, a middle ground can involve asking your team to cc or forward you certain key e-mails. When doing this, be transparent about your reasoning—explain that it's not about a lack of trust but simply a way to keep you informed so you're not playing catch-up or doubling up on tasks when you return. Put it in real terms: "To be clear, I trust you and don't want you to feel you need to include me in every communication to cover for yourself. But if something comes up that you think I should know about, I can look at the e-mails and know that it's handled, or we can talk about the next steps together." This lets your team know you trust them to handle the day-to-day while you're just staying in the loop to make the transition back smoother.

Looking forward to your own time off? Now, before you start planning your next trip (which you should!), consider how you can support your team in taking theirs.

RIPPLE EFFECTS: SUPPORTING YOUR TEAM'S TIME OFF

It's not enough to just tell your team to take time off—you have to create and maintain a culture that supports and encourages it. Remember, if your actions don't match your words, your team will feel pressured to stay on even when they desperately need a break. If you're constantly working through your own vacations, sending e-mails late at night, or never fully disconnecting, you're setting an unspoken standard that taking time off isn't realistic. To truly lead by example, you need to make taking time off a supported expectation, not just a check-the-box talking point.

Start with actionable steps to create that environment where taking time off is normal and respected. Openly discuss the importance of recharging, not only for yourself but also for the team. Regularly check in with your team about whether they've taken time off recently and scheduling it in the future, especially if it seems like they've been going full throttle for a while. Some employees may need a gentle reminder to prioritize their own well-being, particularly in high-pressure environments where it can feel like being "always on" is a sign of your value.

But remember that it often takes more than a "gentle reminder" to get your team to actually use their time off. Your team may hear you encouraging breaks and still think, *That would be nice, but it's just not realistic.* By encouraging your team to recharge, discussing how to balance time off with work, and modeling that behavior yourself, you demonstrate that recharging isn't just a luxury—it's something that can make you more successful at work and is part of a sustainable career.

Be realistic about the constraints your team may face. If your team has limited vacation time or operates in an environment where taking time off feels difficult, talk about that and explore ways they can still take time off. It's important to communicate up front about peak times when vacations are harder to accommodate so that expectations are clear. This is when, in hiring and onboarding, it's so important to be transparent about those aspects. Discuss these busy periods to avoid surprises later, like a new hire expecting a nonnegotiable vacation right in the middle of your busiest season. While most situations can be worked through, addressing them early helps prevent stress and misunderstandings.

If you have the opportunity to influence senior leadership, consider advocating for policies that promote realistic time off for your team. Use data to support your case (refer back to the insights from the beginning of this chapter, showing how vacation time actually boosts team productivity). For example, you might propose implementing company-wide holidays during periods that are already slow. This approach can be a win-win for the organization: Enabling everyone to take a break at the same time can reflect reality (when team members in the office may be thinking, *Why am I actually here?*) and helps the entire team return refreshed without facing a backlog. Additionally, offering structured breaks like this can serve as a powerful tool when you're hiring (or "attracting top talent," which may resonate better with senior leadership).

When influencing senior leadership isn't feasible (if you're thinking, *I know for a fact that conversation wouldn't go over well*), shift your focus to supporting your team within the current limitations. Encourage them to take shorter, meaningful breaks, such as half-days or extended weekends, to recharge even if they can't take longer time off. For those in office settings, you could also implement "no-meeting" days to ease daily demands and give your team the mental space they need. Even small adjustments like these can help your team recharge and maintain engagement.

Along with intentionally prioritizing time off and recognizing when busy periods may make planned time off challenging or nearly impossible, it's essential to work collaboratively to establish a fair and balanced approach to scheduling time off. For example, if you have a policy that only one employee can be off at once and one employee consistently gets the first week of summer off every year, it can lead to frustration or resentment among others. To avoid this, have an open discussion about how time off is allocated and how the team can work together to ensure fairness. Be open to different suggestions—while ideally, you might want to avoid multiple team members being out at once, it's important to be prepared for that possibility. As we'll explore in the next chapter, there will be times when multiple team members are going to be out anyway, due to sickness or personal needs. You don't want to be the kind of manager who makes employees feel like they have to call in sick just to take a break. When you're up front about the best times to take time off and are flexible when you can be, you build trust and transparency within the team.

A great way to make candid conversations about time off a regular part of your team's culture is to introduce the topic into team meetings. For example, you could add an agenda item to an upcoming meeting called "How We Can Actually Be 'Off' During Time Off." You might phrase it differently, but it's the kind of discussion that team members actually want to attend. For shift-based environments like manufacturing, retail, or health care, this can be a quick topic during daily huddles. During the meeting, share how you personally prepare for time off and invite others to share their tips as well. This not only encourages real, honest conversation but also allows everyone to learn from each other's experiences. Consider having a team member take notes and compile the key points into a reference guide for future planning. If your team uses automated tools (like AI for meeting notes), you might even streamline this process with minimal effort.

One important point: As part of the discussion, be sure to emphasize the need to find and share practical approaches that help balance time off while ensuring things don't fall through the cracks. For example, in a session like this, a colleague admitted,

"I just delete all the unread e-mails I got when I was out. I figure that if it's important enough, they'll resend it." While that might feel like a quick fix, explain that it's not the best long-term move—what if an important update, deadline, or decision is buried in those e-mails?

This is a great moment to use the **Pause-Consider-Act** framework with your team. First, acknowledge that coming back to a full inbox can be overwhelming. Then, consider alternative ways to manage it—like setting aside time to catch up on e-mails, using filters, or having a colleague flag anything urgent. Finally, act on a strategy that keeps things manageable without missing something important.

Speaking of the **Pause-Consider-Act** framework, this is a perfect example of it in action: pausing to plan, considering what your team needs to hear, and acting to communicate it effectively both to the team as a whole and to individuals. You can use this opportunity to reinforce the importance of time off, remind team members of the process to request it, set clear expectations for coverage before and after time off, and follow up with individual check-ins.

UNDERSTANDING YOUR TEAM AS INDIVIDUALS

Supporting time off isn't just a talking point for team meetings—it's about actions you can take to create a team that cares about their work and wants to stick around and grow with your organization because they feel valued as individuals. A big part of that is recognizing and respecting that each team member is an individual and has unique needs and wants. Not everyone has the same needs when it comes to time off. Some might be focused on advancing their careers and eager to gain as much experience as possible, while others may rely on extra shifts to make ends meet. The key is finding the right balance between their need for work and their need for rest.

Shift Settings

In a shift-based setting, such as health care, retail, or food service, some team members may want—and ask for—more shifts for financial reasons. That can include times when they're saving for something in particular, like a house or a future vacation. So, when you discuss the importance of taking time off, they might think, *That's great for others, but I need to work more.* Have an open conversation with your team members about their needs and find ways to support them, like keeping them informed about available shifts. Let them know you're there to help them achieve their financial goals, but also encourage them to recharge when they're ready. You can make that conversation easier for everyone by addressing it in a team meeting: "Time off matters, but I also know there are times when you're looking for extra shifts. If you ever want to pick up more, just let me know. I can't guarantee anything, but I'll do my best to make it work and keep you in mind if we need coverage."

Office Settings

In more corporate settings, especially in start-ups or professional services firms, the expectation to work more than 60 hours a week (or late/odd hours) can often be part of the culture, even if it's an unspoken one. This creates an environment where time off feels less like a benefit and more like an illusion—something that's talked about but never truly an option. While the demands of these environments might create the sense that constant work is necessary and expected, this working style can easily lead your best team members to burn out. It's especially important to encourage time off as a critical part of long-term success, even in these high-pressure situations.

You can, and should, have honest conversations about how excessive long hours can have impacts on the quality of your work and your health.[4] But that can also be met with the same skepticism I've talked about. So make it more realistic. Highlight team members who have taken time off and still succeeded in their careers.

The "How We Can Actually Be 'Off' During Time Off" sessions I mentioned earlier can be especially helpful here, whether you have those just with your team or advocate for them to be offered across the organization. These conversations can be game-changers. By doing this, you're reducing your team's stress while also opening the door for innovative ideas that support both individual growth and your organization's long-term goals.

In Any Setting

Whatever your work environment, people's needs and priorities often reflect what's happening in their lives outside of work. Some may focus on picking up extra hours to hit financial goals, while others might prioritize spending more time with family or taking time to recharge. It all comes back to having open, honest conversations about work-life balance and taking time off. By encouraging your team to share their priorities, you can better support them in meaningful ways.

This shouldn't mean forcing employees to make a choice between a pay raise and paid time off; rather, it's about recognizing that priorities shift over time. Some team members may feel like their value is measured only in hours worked, but that's not the case. Flexibility and understanding in your approach show them that their contributions go beyond just time on the clock. When you meet employees where they are—whether they're focused on finances, career growth, or personal well-being—you create a workplace where they feel truly valued. And when you consistently support your team in ways that matter to them, you build a group that's more engaged, committed, and excited to stick around.

RESPECTING ROLES WHILE COVERING FOR OTHERS

Just as you'll need to be thoughtful in planning your time off, your team members need to approach theirs strategically, too. You can support them by helping them plan ahead so they can step away without worrying, knowing the team has their back (or inbox, as the case may be). That also means setting them up to return the favor when it's someone else's turn. Whether it's delegating tasks, making sure responsibilities are covered, or keeping everyone clear on who's handling what, a little preparation goes a long way in making time off work smoothly for everyone.

Before their vacation, think about any information or access you (and others) might need so you won't have to interrupt them. A question like, "If we have questions about [insert topic], where can I find the answers so we don't bother you while you're away?" encourages them to think ahead and provide a solution before they leave. If a situation arises where you absolutely need to reach out, be transparent about the reason. Getting a random message out of nowhere can make people wonder whether you actually need something or are just checking up on their work. You might be thinking, *I don't have time in my day to be checking up on people like that!* But plenty of employees worry that's exactly what's happening when they're out. A simple heads-up, like saying you just need quick access to something, can go a long way in reassuring them that you're not micromanaging their work.

By actively supporting your team in taking time off and being intentional about how and when you communicate, you're building trust in a way that likely matters more to them than you might think. You probably don't need to ask your team, "Have you ever had a manager who helped you take time off?" to know that most haven't had that experience. But with your approach, they finally will. When your team feels genuinely supported in taking time away, you're setting a positive example for how time off should be managed, and building strong relationships that make the whole team work better. Because the way you take time off directly affects how you show up when you're back on.

BEYOND VACATION: ENSURING OFF-HOURS ARE TRULY OFF

Have you ever taken the time to really think about your work habits and the expectations you have for others around working hours? Thanks to technology, it's easier than ever to reach out to your team at any time, but that doesn't mean it's always necessary or even the best approach. A good rule to follow is: If you wouldn't go to their house at 10:00 P.M. to ask them a question, then think twice about sending them a chat, message, or e-mail. It's about respecting boundaries and recognizing that just because you have access to instant communication doesn't mean it should be used outside of regular work hours.

I've heard a lot of pushback to this, and I understand. I've received comments like, "That's ridiculous. I can choose to send it when it's convenient for me, and they can read it when it's convenient for them." However, as a manager, it's critical to keep in mind the power dynamic in your relationship, especially in communication. As a leader, your messages carry weight, even when you don't intend them to. For instance, sending an e-mail late at night or on a weekend, even if you say "it's not urgent," can create a sense of pressure on your team. If you send an e-mail at 10:00 A.M. on a Saturday, even if you mean for them to read it on Monday, it may still take up their mental space over the weekend (and they may lose sleep about it on both Saturday *and* Sunday nights). They might worry about it, or feel tempted or even obligated to respond earlier than they should. And if you've ever woken up to a slew of 2:00 A.M. e-mails from your manager, especially when they're in the same time zone, it can create stress that doesn't bode well for the day—or longer.

How you work now can directly impact your own career path. Remember, succession planning works both ways. Just like when hiring for a role on your team, when it's your turn to move up, you want someone to be excited about stepping into your position. But if your job looks overwhelming—endless hours, e-mails at all times of day and night—that excitement (and interest) might disappear fast. And if no one on your team wants the role, you could find yourself stuck in a lengthy search for an external hire, meaning you may have to keep doing your current job *and* preparing for your next role until a replacement is found. Even then, there's no guarantee the new hire will stick around. They might start, only to quickly realize why no one internally wanted the job in the first place, putting you right back at square one.

It's why seemingly small habits can matter. Using tools like "scheduled send" for e-mails and chats helps protect your team's personal time and reinforces a culture where work doesn't bleed into personal hours unless absolutely necessary. Another impactful habit is being intentional about how you communicate, starting with small details like spelling names correctly and providing clear context in your messages. For example, instead of sending a vague, jarring e-mail like, "Call me—thx," you could say, "Hi [insert name], I wanted to chat for five minutes about a question on the report for the client meeting so I can explain it correctly. It looks like you're free at 3 P.M., but let me know if that doesn't work." If you've never thought about how different it can feel to receive those two messages, I guarantee your team has. These simple shifts can have significant impacts on your team's mindset and, in turn, their work.

It's not just about *your* habits—your team's communication practices are equally important, and you play a key role in helping them understand the why and how of effective communication. Holding sessions with your team to discuss workplace communication norms is something many leaders overlook, but it can be incredibly helpful. For instance, you can pose questions like, "When you need help from a colleague, how do you typically approach them? How can you consider your own preferences and theirs to make the process more productive and efficient?" This can lead to a valuable and practical conversation about expectations, improving collaboration among your team and with others.

These discussions are a great chance to introduce helpful tips and tools that you'll implement, like using scheduled send, emphasizing the importance of addressing colleagues by name (their properly spelled name), and providing context in messages. You can even use these meetings for practical discussions about real-life scenarios, like what to do if someone isn't responding when you urgently need an answer (and discuss what "urgently" really means). These conversations can help establish shared guidelines that balance consideration and respect for others while getting important work done efficiently. A lot of team members might not have thought about these things before, but you can help them start noticing, and even make them part of their everyday work. And just like **Pause-Consider-Act** teaches, you can always tailor them to the unique circumstances of your team.

WHEN YOUR TEAM WORKS ACROSS DIFFERENT TIME ZONES

One unique challenge is working across different time zones. Earlier, I talked about how to approach team meetings, but there's more to consider, especially when managing a global team. It's also a great way for your team to pick up things they never even knew before— different working styles, cultural perspectives, and fresh ideas that can make everyone better. But even if you're just working with colleagues spread across a large country, different time zones can make "working hours" a complicated topic.

When your team works across different time zones, relying on tools like scheduled send isn't always practical. With global teams, working hours might overlap briefly, if at all. That's why it's so important to be intentional about communication and clear about expectations. If you send a message outside someone's typical working hours and need a response, make it clear they're only expected to reply during their own working hours. Adding language to your e-mail signature can go a long way. For example: "Please note, I work with a global team across various time zones. While this e-mail was sent during my working hours, there's no expectation for you to respond outside of yours."

This kind of clarity can help your team take advantage of the benefits of asynchronous communication—like e-mail—that allows global colleagues to collaborate effectively without always requiring everyone to "jump on a quick call." You might be used to "collaborative" work, meaning everyone meets at the same time, but with tools like shared documents and screen sharing, you can still get everyone's input without cutting into their personal time or sleep. By establishing these expectations and using available technology, you give your team certainty and a chance to add their input, and you do it when they're refreshed rather than rushing to finish so they can get to bed.

CHECKLIST FOR ENCOURAGING BALANCE WHILE WORKING

Using the **Pause-Consider-Act** framework for work practices is important, but it can feel challenging when you're busy. Here are five tips to remember, regardless of your team's work environment.

1. **Encourage intentional time management.**
    Engage your team in open discussions about how they approach and manage their time. Ask how they navigate the balance between completing their work and taking time to recharge. Be mindful of these conversations—some of your team members might hold back on sharing great ideas because they're afraid it'll just lead to more work as a "reward." Let your team know that sharing ideas (and being efficient) doesn't automatically mean more work piled on them. Instead, find ways to recognize their input that feel supportive and encouraging, not like a punishment.

2. **Get real about balance—including its benefits.**
    Use these conversations to guide your team in making decisions they're likely to encounter. Talk about examples of situations that require urgent attention and how to escalate those appropriately, as well as how team members can be reachable when needed, without feeling like they have to be "on" 24/7. Likewise, share examples of

what can wait and how to communicate that effectively (including how to involve you if it helps set expectations with others). In the same way, you can celebrate colleagues who advance in their careers while also taking regular vacations, and recognize those who achieve success while maintaining balance in their day-to-day work. Ask them to talk about how they do it so others can learn.

3. **Model balance and time management.** Don't just say it—model it. Show your team it's okay to disconnect by truly stepping away during your off-hours. If you do need to step in for an issue, take the opportunity to explain how you addressed it and share any tips for handling similar situations in the future. For example, if you've been repeatedly receiving off-hours communications about the same issue, work with your team to brainstorm solutions, such as creating a resource like an FAQ or a quick-reference guide. This can help team members find answers independently, reducing the need for after-hours interruptions and creating a more self-sufficient, efficient workflow.

4. **Respect working hours.** Be considerate of your team members' working hours, especially if they're in different time zones. Avoid off-day and off-hour e-mails unless absolutely necessary, and take advantage of scheduling tools and other asynchronous technology when possible.

5. **Provide flexibility where you can.** If your team is working across different schedules or time zones and occasionally handling things outside their usual hours, acknowledge that effort and offer flexibility in return. For example, you might say, "Thanks for jumping on those early calls this week—feel free to wrap up early on Friday and get a head start on your weekend." Recognizing their time and giving them room to recharge goes a long way.

LEAD BY EXAMPLE

These leadership lessons aren't just something I recommend to others. They're deeply personal to me. At the start of this chapter, I shared a story about a vacation that was supposed to be relaxing but turned into the exact opposite. I couldn't change what happened, but I could (and did) use the **Pause-Consider-Act** framework to think intentionally about how I wanted to approach things moving forward, and act on it.

In my next role, a colleague and I made an agreement (and, importantly, a plan) to cover for each other during time off. We followed the exact steps outlined here—meeting in advance of our time off to update each other on key projects, share important e-mails, and ensure we could fully disconnect during our vacations. I'll never forget the feeling when, for the first time in my professional career, I took a trip without my work laptop. My bag and my mind felt lighter than they had in years. When I returned, I was excited to catch her up on my vacation, and she filled me in on everything I'd missed.

This experience didn't just change how I felt on and after that trip; it completely shifted my approach to work and life. I carried this mindset into my work as a manager, encouraging team members (often for the first time) to think about how they recharged, whether on travel or in their daily work. It's now a cornerstone of my work training managers and organizations, and the tips in this book are built on those same principles.

It is completely possible for you—and your teams—to get work done and live a full life outside of work. Taking time off and recharging isn't just about stepping away for a vacation. It's about setting a standard for your team, modeling healthy work habits, and empowering them to take ownership when you're not there. When you follow the **Pause-Consider-Act** framework, you create a plan that allows both you and your team to succeed without burnout. Remember, your actions set the tone for your team's actions; by prioritizing rest and balance, you create a culture where everyone can perform at their best.

Questions for Self-Reflection

- **How do I prepare for time off, and what can I do differently to ensure I can truly disconnect?**

  Reflect on how effective your current process is for stepping away from work and what adjustments you can make to improve your ability to fully recharge.

- **Do I communicate boundaries around work hours clearly to my team, or do my actions send mixed signals?**

  Consider whether the way you communicate matches what you're telling your team to do—and whether your actions might be unintentionally pushing them toward overwork.

- **When was the last time I checked in with my team about their time off or work-life balance? How did I support their needs?**

  Consider how often you actively engage with your team about their time off and well-being, and evaluate whether you've provided the right level of support.

- **Am I utilizing tools like scheduled send to respect my team's off-hours, or do I unintentionally create pressure for them to respond outside of work time?**

  Reflect on whether your communication habits truly respect your team's personal time, and think about how tools like scheduled send can help manage expectations.

- **How am I encouraging my team to share their individual priorities and needs with me, and what steps can I take to support their work-life balance more effectively?**

  Think about the ways you create honest conversations around personal and professional priorities, and explore how you can better support their individual needs.

Chapter 9

Real-Life Situations

Putting the Framework into Action

As a manager, you're constantly trying to get things "right"—from hiring the right people and delegating effectively, to ensuring accountability and supporting your team, all while driving results. It can feel like the challenges never stop, but the **Pause-Consider-Act** formula gives you a framework to approach these situations thoughtfully. It helps you set clear expectations, build trust, and guide your team through tricky moments. It also shows them why their work matters and how to balance it with the need to recharge.

If you're thinking, *I still have questions*, don't worry—this book isn't over. We've already covered why having a clear, practical approach is so essential for the situations you'll face as a manager. But managing people is never one-size-fits-all, and unexpected challenges will always arise. The key is learning to expect the unexpected, and in this chapter, we'll talk about specific situations and how to navigate them.

Before we get into specific situations, take a moment to think back to when you first became a manager. You were probably great at your job, excelling in your role, and the natural next step was to become a manager. You got promoted, celebrated, and told how "exciting" this new role would be. It felt great—receiving the offer, sharing the news with friends and family, and updating your new title on LinkedIn. You may have even been flooded with congratulatory messages, as if you'd won a prize.

And you did—because managing people is a privilege, giving you the opportunity to impact their lives in ways you might never have imagined. But that's also where the challenge lies. You may not have fully understood what being a manager is like, at least not before stepping into the role. In Chapter 4, I talked about how important it is to make sure candidates have a realistic view of a role before accepting an offer. You may not have had that. The reality of managing people is often different from what most people expect. All of a sudden, your job shifts from *doing* the work to managing and guiding others to get *their* work done. Sometimes you have to do both—managing a team and your own workload. It's not easy, especially when you're balancing emotions, navigating conflicts, and handling unexpected demands along the way.

Difficult conversations and decisions are part of the job; they're inevitable. They can take many forms: a discussion about performance, addressing a personal issue impacting a team member, or dealing with something unexpected at the worst possible time. What feels challenging to one person might seem simple to another, but as a manager, it's essential to approach these moments with care and intentionality. That's where the **Pause-Consider-Act** framework comes in—it can help you stay grounded and navigate these situations thoughtfully and effectively.

SHOULD HR HANDLE IT?

While difficult conversations can be one of the most uncomfortable parts of management, they're often the moments that can make or break your leadership. Things will go wrong, but you can help get it back on track. You might be thinking, *Why do we have to get involved at all—shouldn't people handle this like adults?* The reality is that ignoring issues doesn't make them go away. They can linger, but with the right approach, you can help resolve them and move the team forward for the better. Because as a manager, your role goes beyond overseeing work; it's about supporting your team and helping them develop the skills to handle challenges effectively. You have a bigger impact on this than you might realize.

Don't worry—not everything is solely your responsibility. While the resources available to you may vary depending on your organization, you're not expected to handle it all alone. So, when a tough conversation comes up, shouldn't you just leave it to the experts? In other words, you might now be wondering, *Why is this on me? Isn't HR supposed to handle "people" issues?*

It's a natural instinct for many managers to turn to HR when faced with a difficult situation, but some managers take that as a cue to step out completely, expecting HR to take over. While there are definitely times when HR should be involved, it's important to pause and consider the best approach for your team member. As we covered earlier in the book, people tend to see situations through the lens of how they're personally impacted, and more often than not, they look to you—not HR—for support. Even in the most difficult moments, your team is counting on you to take the lead.

When HR steps in, the conversation can take on a more formal tone, which sometimes intimidates team members or escalates the situation unnecessarily. Team members typically come to you because they trust you. If you send them to HR too quickly—especially without explaining why—it can feel like you're brushing them off or avoiding the issue, even if that's not what you mean to do. That's why it's important to assess each situation with care and think intentionally before deciding how to proceed.

Consider the nature of the issue: Is it something you can handle directly, or does it require HR's expertise? The employee handbook can offer some guidance, but in many cases, the expectations aren't always clear. If you're unsure, your HR team can likely help you understand what's expected of you and when you need to involve others. It's a good idea to connect with your HR team (perhaps right after finishing this chapter) to clarify which situations need their involvement, what they expect managers to handle, and how they can support you from behind the scenes. Building a good relationship with HR can help you see them as more than just a rule-making department. They have a lot of experience with "people" challenges and can help you understand the different options and what might happen. They're there to support you, whether you're handling a conversation on your own or working with them to find the best approach.

Finally, when you act, it's important to recognize that while you'll handle many people-related challenges, some situations require HR or other leaders to step in. There may also be information or context you're not aware of that impacts how an issue should be resolved. For example, if the situation involves legal requirements, a potential policy violation, or a sensitive personal matter, HR may need to be directly involved, instead of supporting you behind the scenes. Almost always, HR would rather have a conversation with you early on about when to loop them in than find out after it's too late.

Having worked in HR (and legal), I've often heard the phrase, "HR's not your friend—they're just there to protect the organization." This comment usually comes from people who haven't worked in HR themselves. In reality, many HR professionals face the same challenges that managers do. While every function has examples of people who may not be suited for the role, most HR teams are made up of good people who are stretched thin, not as well trained as they'd like to be (or as others expect them to be), and whose most impactful work often happens behind the scenes by advocating for better performance management, pushing for development opportunities, and trying to build a case for change (but not being the ones to actually make the decisions).

Even from a skeptical perspective, HR rarely benefits from treating people poorly—it usually makes their job harder. This book isn't about convincing you to view HR differently, but about showing how you, as a manager, can strengthen your leadership and support your team by partnering with HR effectively. Rather than avoiding HR out of mistrust, understanding when and how to collaborate with them ensures that issues are handled in a way that protects both the employee and the organization. Building this partnership allows for smoother resolutions and stronger support for everyone involved.

So, what about the real-life scenarios you'll encounter? Just as I encourage you not to simply tell your team, "Go ask HR,"* I'll walk you through examples of how to handle these situations. Each one will be grounded in the **Pause-Consider-Act** framework so you can see exactly how to put it into practice.

One of the most important things to remember is that there's no magic potion for management. You won't always have all the answers, and that's okay. What matters is having options and knowing how to approach each situation. It's about how you handle the conversation, how you listen, and how you guide your team through the challenge. The **Pause-Consider-Act** framework provides a clear method to help you do just that. Now we'll explore how this approach applies to some common situations you might encounter as a manager or have already faced.

HOW TO START ALMOST ANY DIFFICULT CONVERSATION

In almost any situation, one of the best first steps is asking questions. But not *only* asking questions, because your team is likely looking for some actual help and guidance, not an interrogation. You might think back to work experiences where someone, perhaps your manager, started a conversation without having all the facts. It *is* possible to recover from that (and we'll cover how in this chapter), but it's much easier to approach things differently from the beginning. Starting with the right approach allows you to gather more information before forming judgments or making decisions.

Asking questions not only helps you understand the other person's perspective but also gives you a moment to pause and slow the conversation, allowing you both time to think. For example, instead of immediately jumping to conclusions or offering solutions, try asking, "Can you walk me through what happened?" or "What's bothering you the most about this?" or "What do you think

---

* If you're wondering what to say instead, example words are, "I can try to help with that. If we need HR's input, I'll make sure we connect with them the right way." This approach reassures your team that you're there to support them, rather than making it feel like you're passing them off.

should happen?" By first focusing on gathering information, you give yourself the space to listen and avoid assumptions that could lead to missteps you might later regret.

This approach matters because it changes the dynamic from a knee-jerk reaction to a more thoughtful response, where you actually have time to consider what to do next. Asking questions gives both sides room to think more clearly and work toward a solution. You'll likely learn information that gives you a better sense of what's going on. Once you understand the situation more clearly, responding with confidence and composure—even in difficult conversations—becomes much easier.

Let's talk through those difficult situations that managers face. Because you don't just need theory—you need real examples of what to do. So, here's what it looks like when those hard moments actually happen, and how you can handle them.

When Your Team Is Short-Staffed

When your team's short-staffed, the immediate reaction is often to buckle down and push through the additional workload ("It is what it is . . . we all just have to step up"). While this might work in the short term, it quickly leads to frustration and burnout. It's important to recognize reality. Your team is already talking about it among themselves—wouldn't you rather be part of the conversation?

Pause and think about the long-term impact on your team's morale and productivity if everyone is stretched too thin. Consider how to prioritize tasks and whether you can delegate work differently, bring in temporary help, or even decide that some things have to wait. Consider how open communication can help here. Managers often worry about overcommunicating, thinking that bringing it up will turn it into a bigger issue than it actually is. But involving the team in the conversation shows them you understand the situation and allows you to gain their valuable input on which tasks are most critical and where each team member feels they can best contribute. Act by holding a team meeting to reassess priorities, making sure that everyone understands which projects need immediate attention and which can be delayed. You can use real examples, such as, "Given our team's current size, if an urgent client request comes in, we might need to pause a lower-priority internal project to get it done. But it's important to first discuss priorities, and clearly communicate the shift—and the reasons behind it—to internal colleagues." Additionally, you can relieve some of the pressure by keeping your own leadership in the loop about the strain on your team and requesting temporary support, or at least setting expectations that productivity may dip due to team capacity.

Example: A manager was feeling overwhelmed by the demands on their short-staffed team after two employees unexpectedly had to take leave. When the rest of the team started venting about taking on the work of their team members, the manager really wanted to say, "Imagine how the people who didn't plan to be out feel? Or me, trying to juggle all of this?! I just need you to stop complaining and get to work."

But instead of saying the first thing that came to mind*—and pushing the team harder—the manager paused and thought about what was really happening. Yes, the team was venting, but it was a mix of frustration, looking out for themselves, and voicing real concerns about how much extra work they might be expected to take on. The manager still needed to be direct about how their reactions were showing up, but leading with some understanding first made it easier to have that conversation.

They held a team meeting and started by addressing the reality: When someone is unexpectedly out, it's easy to immediately think, *How is this going to affect my workload?* That's a normal reaction. But it's also important to step back and recognize that life happens. People get sick, have emergencies, or need time away. As a team, part of the job is to support each other and figure out how to adjust when those situations come up.

From there, they worked with the group to figure out what absolutely needed to be covered, what could shift, and how to divide things up. The manager got the team's input on priorities and reached

---

* I've talked a lot in this book about "reactions," because you're human, and they're completely natural. But as a leader, what often matters is how you respond. That's where *Pause-Consider-Act* comes in. Instead of reacting in the moment, you're giving yourself space to step back and make sure you respond in a way that meets people where they are and helps guide them to where you need them to be.

out to leadership to secure temporary help for one key project that couldn't be delayed.

By pausing to talk with and involve the team, the manager didn't ignore their initial reaction to team members hearing the news about others being out and immediately thinking about how it would affect *them*. But instead of letting that frustration build, the manager acknowledged it, eased some of the pressure, and had a real conversation about how teams support each other when life happens . . . things rarely go exactly how we all initially plan.

When an Employee Is Always Late

When you have an employee who is consistently late, it can be tempting to jump straight to warnings, write-ups, or even letting them go. But it's important to pause and think about the underlying reasons for their lateness—what's going on, and what's the impact? Consider whether there's something outside of work affecting their ability to get in on time. Also, does their lateness genuinely disrupt the work or team, or is it less significant, especially if they're staying later to make up for it? You might assume they're late because they don't take their job seriously, but in reality, they could be juggling a tough personal situation along with work.

Then, act, which often starts with having a conversation. Remember when I mentioned that asking questions is the first step? Now, imagine you have a team member who's become consistently late, and instead of asking what's going on, you immediately say, "Your workday starts at eight. If you're not here on time, I have to assume you don't want the job."

Let's imagine two different responses.

First, picture this: They roll their eyes and say, "I'm only a few minutes late—it's not that big of a deal. I'm getting my work done."

Now, picture a different response: They tear up and say, "My daughter's school just changed drop-off to 7:55, and I'm doing my best to get here as fast as I can. I've even enrolled her in after-school care so I can stay late to make up the time."

Two completely different reactions—and understandably, your response as a manager would be different in each situation. But if you start the conversation with curiosity rather than assumptions, it can change how both scenarios play out. A simple, non-defensive question like, "Can you help me understand what's making it hard to get here by eight?" opens the door to a real conversation, no matter what the initial reaction is.

Some jobs truly require set coverage. But others allow for more flexibility. And this is one of those rare times I'll put my lawyer hat on and say: If you were on the witness stand and your only reason for saying someone can't start at 8:15 instead of 8:00 was, "Because I said so," you know who wouldn't find that convincing? A jury.

Taking a moment to pause, consider, and ask questions allows you to respond with fairness and empathy, while still addressing the issue effectively. It encourages—and communicates—understanding rather than jumping straight to a reprimand. You might instead say, "I've noticed you've been running late a lot lately, and I just want to check in—what's going on? Is there something I can help with?" This addresses what you've been seeing and opens the door for potential solutions. It also helps you tackle the issue right away, rather than letting it drag on and addressing it long after it first happened. Or you could try an AI prompt like: *"What's a good way to talk to my team member about being late, so I can explain why being on time matters and also understand what's been getting in the way?"*

Approaching the conversation with empathy allows you to reinforce why being on time matters, while also recognizing that employees have real lives outside of work. It's easy to assume someone doesn't care (and sometimes that's true) but often there are legitimate challenges they're trying to navigate. As a manager, your job is to strike the right balance: setting clear expectations while recognizing that people have real lives outside of work.

Example: At a medical center, an 8 A.M. shift required full coverage due to health care staffing ratios. When one team member started showing up late nearly every day, the manager chose to have a conversation instead of making assumptions. The employee explained that their parent had been admitted into the hospital for an extended stay, and they were trying to visit before and after work within the limited patient visiting hours. While the employee said they understood the importance of punctuality and offered to cut their visits short, the manager took a different approach, asking whether anyone on the earlier shift would be open to staying 30 minutes later each day to ensure coverage. Two team members volunteered, happy to pick up extra hours. This simple adjustment kept coverage intact, supported multiple employees, and demonstrated the manager's empathy and problem-solving mindset.

When You Really Don't Want to Have a Conversation

Sometimes, when you notice an issue with a team member, it's tempting to not say anything. This may be because they're a strong performer and you worry that addressing it could push them away. Or they may not be, but you're hoping that it will resolve on its own, or they'll just quit. But whatever's happening doesn't just impact them—or you. Avoiding the conversation often lets the problem grow, impacting both the individual and the rest of the team. The good news? For any conversation—whether it's about performance, attendance, or workload—there's a wide range of options between saying nothing and driving someone away. When handled with empathy and a focus on solutions, these conversations can strengthen relationships, uncover underlying issues, and create a path forward, without making the conversation uncomfortable.

Example 1: A manager in an office environment noticed that one of their top team members had been missing deadlines and submitting incomplete work—a big change from their usual high standards. The manager was reluctant to say anything, worried that addressing it could lead the employee to quit. The company had just announced a hiring freeze, so if this person quit, not only would it be a huge loss to the team, but also they likely wouldn't be able to replace them.

After weeks of mounting frustration and grumbling from other team members, the manager decided to have a conversation. They approached the employee with empathy, saying, "I've noticed your workload seems to be overwhelming lately, and I wanted to check in—how are things going? Is there something we can adjust to make it more manageable?"

The employee admitted they were struggling to balance their workload because they'd taken on extra responsibilities after another co-worker left—that hiring freeze was causing stress among the team. They hesitated to speak up, worried it would make them seem incapable and that nothing would change anyway. Eventually, they opened up, admitting that they were considering leaving because they didn't see a path forward. Realizing the risk of burnout and turnover, the manager took action. They gathered data on workload distribution, highlighted the impact on team morale and productivity, and made a case to senior leadership about the long-term financial risks of continuing without additional support. By framing it as both a retention and a performance issue, they secured approval to hire an additional team member. In the meantime, they worked with leadership to reprioritize tasks and redistribute projects to lighten the load. This not only eased the employee's stress but also reinforced that leadership valued their team's well-being.

By addressing the issue instead of staying silent, the manager not only supported the employee but also advocated for solutions that benefited the entire team. While staying quiet may have felt easier in the short term, taking action showed trust, addressed issues, and prevented problems from snowballing. These conversations don't have to be all or nothing—they can involve practical questions like, "How would we make the best use of an additional team member?" or "If hiring isn't an option, what adjustments could help make your workload more manageable?" Addressing it early opens the door to solutions, because waiting until others have left only makes the conversation even harder.

Example 2: Let's revisit the earlier example of a manager whose employee started coming in late because their child's school start time had changed. But there's a twist. This time, instead of addressing it right away, the manager let it slide—for months. Other team members began noticing and questioning why one person seemed to have a different set of expectations. Frustration built quietly until someone accused the manager of playing favorites. *Favorites?! The opposite!* thought the manager, who was now frustrated about not bringing it up earlier and fed up. The next day, instead of addressing it calmly, they waited at the team member's desk and, when they showed up, angrily announced, "The start time was fifteen minutes ago."

Now, the team member was caught off guard. They wondered, *Why are you just now saying something? Is something else going on?* The delay left them feeling defensive and mistrustful, because the manager's frustration seemed to come out of nowhere. This highlights why it's important to address issues promptly and directly. The longer you wait, the harder it becomes to have a productive conversation, because the delay itself can become part of the problem.

So, what can you say if you're thinking of a situation that you might now want to address but want to prevent it from spiraling? In those situations, it's still important to address it while also acknowledging the delay. One option: "I should have brought this up a while ago, but I didn't—that's on me. I want to check in now and see whether there's anything I might not be aware of?" This acknowledges your delay, sets the tone for an honest and empathetic conversation, and gives the employee space to share their perspective without feeling attacked.

When There's a Negative Team Member

When managing a team member who's consistently negative, it's easy to feel frustrated and think, *Why can't they just be happy to have a job?* But this is a moment where you need to pause and reflect on why they might feel this way. Consider whether there's something deeper driving their negativity. Do they even know how it seems to others? Are they overwhelmed? Do they feel unappreciated or disconnected from their work? It's possible their negativity stems from feeling undervalued or overworked, and as a manager, you might not immediately realize the pressure they're under.

When you act, initiate a conversation with empathy. You might say, "I've noticed you seem frustrated lately. I could be wrong, but I wanted to check in and see if so, what's going on? How can I help?" By approaching the issue with curiosity rather than frustration (and by asking how you can help them, not leave it on them alone to fix), you open the door for productive dialogue. It's also an opportunity to explore whether there are structural issues affecting morale and how you can better support your team.

Example: A manager was frustrated with a team member who constantly complained during meetings. Instead of reacting immediately, they took a moment to reflect and then had a one-on-one conversation to better understand the employee's concerns. The employee said they'd been working long hours without hearing any acknowledgment. They shared examples of when they'd stayed late or missed personal events, questioning whether it was even worth it, because it felt like no one noticed or cared. The manager realized they'd been relying heavily on this employee and assumed everything was fine simply because the employee hadn't said otherwise.

The truth was, the manager had taken the employee's hard work for granted. Realizing this, they started making a real effort to check in regularly, and not just with that employee, but with the whole team. They also made a point to publicly recognize good work while still giving constructive feedback when needed. Along the way, they had an honest conversation with the employee about how their voice carried weight and how their energy—whether positive or negative—often set the tone for the team. Over time, the employee started opening up more and even became a strong, productive voice in team meetings.

When You Explain Something for the Hundredth Time

You've likely been there—explaining something to a team member over and over again, and they just aren't getting it. In these moments, you might very well be frustrated, thinking, *What a waste of time!* But think about it differently. It's crucial to pause and reflect on what might be causing the disconnect. Remember that it's better to recognize the lack of understanding now rather than when it's too late. Consider whether the challenge could be about how the information is being communicated or whether the employee might respond better to a different teaching method. Maybe they learn better with visuals, or perhaps they're confused but afraid to ask for more clarification.

When you act, think about adjusting your approach to help make the information stick—because it's not enough for them to know how to do it when you're standing right there or sharing your screen. They need to feel confident doing it on their own. Part of that is painting the picture up front, so they're not just hearing what to do, but actually thinking through how they'll do it themselves.

You can work that right into your talking points by saying something like, "It seems like this hasn't fully clicked yet. Let's walk through it together; I want to make sure you feel ready to handle this when I'm not right there beside you."

If you've been explaining it the same way and catch yourself thinking, *This should really make sense by now,* it may be time to switch it up. Walk them through it again, but this time, have them actually do it while you observe. Say something like, "I want to make sure I've explained this clearly and that you feel comfortable doing it on your own. Why don't you walk me through it now and I'll watch and afterward give you feedback, but only after you've tried it."

That way, they're practicing in real time and you can catch any confusion before they're expected to handle it solo. This not only helps you pinpoint where the misunderstanding is happening, but it also builds their confidence to handle it without constant guidance. Taking a little extra time up front (or right after noticing mistakes) can help prevent bigger misunderstandings or having to repeat the same conversation later. Showing patience and trying a different way of explaining things can often make the difference, helping employees feel supported and capable rather than frustrated or discouraged.

Example: A manager kept explaining the same process multiple times to an employee, but they kept making mistakes. Despite feeling frustrated, the manager took time to sit with the employee and saw they were taking detailed notes, because they liked to refer to a written guide. The manager initially thought to offer to create a guide for the employee, but instead reached out to IT to see whether there were any training tools available. That's when they discovered the company had software that let managers record a process on their computer, automatically turning it into a video with step-by-step written and visual instructions. The manager gave it a try, and finally, the employee got it.

Not only did this solve the immediate issue, but it also ended up benefiting the whole team. The manager began using the tool to train other employees, making learning more efficient and saving time. Team members even started creating guides for new hires to help them get up to speed more quickly. By shifting their approach to fit how the employee learned best, the manager didn't just solve a problem; they understood different approaches and introduced a resource that made work easier for everyone.

When You're Trying to Get Your Team to Care

Getting and keeping your team engaged—whether in person or remote—can be one of the biggest challenges for a manager. If everyone's quiet, it's understandable to feel frustrated. Your first instinct might be to add more meetings or check-ins to spark conversation or reinforce accountability, but that can sometimes backfire. Instead, pause and assess the current situation. Are team members simply feeling disconnected? Rather than just increasing communication, consider whether the real need is to create more *meaningful* connections.

Instead of just adding more meetings, take a step back and think about how your team is really connecting with one another. If everything feels transactional—just checking things off the to-do list or ticking boxes—it's easy for team members to feel disconnected on a personal level. If people feel like work is just moving from one meeting to the next, and back to work, they likely won't try to build connections.

When you act, recognize that building connections takes time. You can set the tone by creating opportunities for genuine interaction. Team members will have different comfort levels when it comes to sharing at work, so it's important to be mindful of that. Start meetings by checking in with your team, or encourage them to check in on each other. Ask, "Do you think we create enough opportunities to get to know each other as colleagues, not just get work done?" Small actions like this can go a long way in making everyone feel more connected at work. These little moments of connection are what turn a group of co-workers into a real team.

Example: A manager noticed that their team wasn't engaging during meetings and assumed that it reflected how they felt about the manager personally, or even about the organization overall.* Instead of reacting, they paused and considered the possibility that team members didn't just feel disconnected from one another—they literally didn't know each other. With the team feeling stretched thin already, the manager didn't want to add meetings just for the sake of it.

To act on this, the manager adjusted the regular team meeting agenda to include a segment called "Something I Can Teach You." During this rotating segment, a team member would briefly share something they were knowledgeable about, whether it was work software shortcuts, travel hacks for finding cheap flights, or even how to make a three-minute dessert. The team loved these informal moments, which gave them a chance to not only learn from each other but also get to know each other better. These small connections helped make meetings more engaging and brought the team closer together.

When No One Turns Their Cameras On

If you're managing remotely, it can be frustrating when no one turns on their cameras, leaving you talking to a screen of blank squares. Your first instinct might be to demand, "Come on, cameras on, team," but pause and consider why team members might be hesitant. Consider whether there's a discomfort with their surroundings, a sense of video call fatigue, or a misunderstanding of what's expected.

When you act, set clear expectations while allowing for reasonable flexibility. You might say, "We generally should have cameras on so we can connect face-to-face. I get that some days it's not possible, and if there's something you'd rather discuss one-on-one, just let me know." Also, give context to help them understand why it

---

* This happens all the time. Just like I've mentioned, people often assume the worst, and that includes you, too. You might think that employee silence reflects how they feel about you, but that's not necessarily the case.

matters: "If we have others joining us—like someone from another team or a senior leader—it's especially important we have cameras on. We all appreciate the flexibility of remote work, but if no one turns their camera on, it can come across as disengagement and raise questions about whether we should be in the office instead." If you're okay with cameras off during internal team meetings, be up front about when you do expect them on, such as for client calls, leadership discussions, or cross-team meetings. This ensures your team knows what's expected and prevents you from having to later explain to a senior leader why everyone's camera was off when they joined the call.

Example: A manager grew frustrated that their team rarely turned on their cameras during video meetings. Instead of reacting, they asked the team why. They learned that some employees felt self-conscious about their home environments, with some calling in from bedrooms or other less-than-ideal spaces, unaware of simple options to change their virtual backgrounds. Others admitted they didn't see a reason to turn their cameras on because the meetings were mostly the manager talking, so they didn't understand why it mattered if they showed their faces.

The manager took action by showing the team how to update or blur their backgrounds and making the meetings more interactive, encouraging participation and discussion. As team members realized what it was like to present to a screen full of blank boxes, they gradually started turning their cameras on and engaging more. By addressing both the technical barriers and the meeting format, the manager created a more collaborative and connected environment where everyone felt more involved.

When Your Visit Puts Pressure on Your Team

If you don't regularly work in the same location as your team, you might decide to plan a visit, especially if you're managing a large team or have a regional role. When you walk in and see everyone looking busy, it's natural to feel flattered or reassured that they're working hard. But pause to think about why they might be putting on their best show. Consider whether they could be going the extra mile to make things look perfect for you as the "boss" to avoid getting in trouble . . . and to get you out of there. If that's the case, are they working extra just to cover up the reality of what it's like day-to-day? Don't you want to understand what things are really like when you're not around?

When you act, address the underlying issue. You might say, "I've noticed that everyone seems to get busier when I walk in. I'm not coming just so I can see what you think I want to see. I don't want you working around the clock to make things look perfect. I want to understand what's really going on, including the challenges you face day-to-day. We can't learn about—or fix—anything by pretending it's not happening." This way, you can get a true sense of what's going on and hear their ideas on how to improve things. And even if you don't catch them scrambling, ask team members, "What solutions would you like to see?" You can't promise you'll be able to act on everything, but you want to hear their ideas. Make sure to reward them for speaking up and sharing their thoughts; it shows you value their input and are open to making positive changes.

Even better, before you visit, identify one or two team members to recognize for their good work. If there's a local manager, ask for suggestions and let them know this is a chance to highlight team members who don't always get the spotlight (so it's not just the #1 salesperson getting all the praise, but also the support team members who also deserve it). This shifts the focus away from the team scrambling to prepare for your arrival and creates an opportunity for you to see the real day-to-day while also making a positive, memorable moment for someone on the team. By taking these actions, you can turn what's often a stressful event—a leadership visit—into something your team looks forward to, all while helping you become a more connected and effective leader.

Example: A senior leader offered to join a team member in an important upcoming client presentation. As the meeting approached, the leader noticed the team member seemed increasingly nervous. Rather than letting the tension build, the leader addressed it head-on: "I get the sense you're feeling a little anxious about me being there. I want you to know I'm here to support you and make sure I understand the situation, including any challenges that might come up. You own this relationship, and I'm not here to talk over you. I'll be here as backup, but I trust you. You know this relationship, and you've got this."

During a prep session before the meeting, the leader noticed the team member had included insights from the client's recent earnings call in the presentation and asked about it. The team member explained they had listened to the call, and the leader praised them for taking the initiative to do that. During the actual meeting, the leader took a supporting role, allowing the team member to lead the discussion and answer questions. Afterward, in the next internal leadership meeting, the manager invited the team member to talk about their experience from the presentation. The manager also shared what they had learned from attending and praised the team member's preparation and effort in front of the entire leadership team. By offering support before and during the meeting, and recognition afterward, the manager turned a potentially stressful situation into a valuable growth opportunity, boosting the team member's confidence and deepening the manager's understanding of the role and client relationships.

When You're Asked to Talk to the Smelly Employee

This is one of those uncomfortable situations that every manager dreads: talking to an employee whose body odor is the talk of . . . well, everyone else. Your first instinct might be to hope the problem goes away on its own, but this is a time to pause. Consider that the employee might not even be aware there's an issue, or they might be dealing with something that they can't easily control. Reflect on how this affects the team and the importance of addressing it respectfully and discreetly, including using it as a lesson for other team members.

When you act, approach the employee privately and with empathy. You could say, "I wanted to have a quick chat with you about something that might feel a bit uncomfortable, but I thought it was important to mention. You have a noticeable body odor, and I want to check in to see if you realized that, and if there's anything we can do to support you." By framing the conversation as concern rather than criticism, you help maintain the person's dignity while addressing the issue. Then, you talk to the others on the team who brought it up to you, acknowledging that it's uncomfortable for them, but it would also likely be humiliating for this team member to know that everyone else was talking about it—just not to them directly. Encourage them to approach you privately next time so that you can address it without making a colleague feel embarrassed.

Example: A manager was approached by multiple team members who expressed concerns about a colleague's body odor. Rather than avoiding the uncomfortable topic, the manager chose to address it privately with the employee. During the conversation, the employee revealed they were dealing with a medical condition and hadn't realized it was affecting others. The manager gently suggested that the employee might want to consult with their health care provider to explore possible solutions. They also reassured the employee that they could either continue the conversation directly or involve HR if that felt more comfortable.

The employee appreciated the manager's understanding and said they preferred to check in with their doctor and then follow up with the manager directly. Ultimately, they were able to identify a solution to help minimize the issue and thanked the manager for their thoughtful and respectful approach to handling the situation.

When Your Best Employee Lets You Down

When a top-performing employee makes a mistake or misses an important deadline, your immediate reaction might be shock or disappointment. It's easy to think, *How could they drop the ball?* But it's crucial to pause and consider that even your best employees will have off days. Someone's "best" can look different depending on the day. They may be feeling overwhelmed, dealing with personal challenges, or just stretched thin. As a manager, how you respond to the mistake can either help the situation feel more bearable—or more terrible.

When you act, approach them with a balance of empathy and accountability. You might say, "I know this isn't typical for you. My job is to ensure the work gets done well and to support you with anything else that might be going on. Is there something happening that I can help with or support you through?" By leading with support rather than blame, you allow the employee to explain what's going on while also making it clear that they're not alone as they bounce back. This not only helps address the immediate issue but also reinforces that you value them and are there for them, through both the best days and the hard ones.

Example: A manager was frustrated when their star employee missed an important client deadline. The manager initially felt let down, but started the conversation by simply asking, "Can you walk me through what happened? I want to understand, not come down on you." The employee was expecting to get fired and became emotional. They explained that they'd been dealing with a family emergency, but they thought they could still get the work done. The manager reminded them that the team existed for a reason—to support each other when needed. Together, the manager and employee smoothed the client issue, and the employee bounced back stronger with even more trust in the manager's leadership.

When You Need to Give Critical Feedback Without Crushing Your Team Member

Providing critical feedback is often uncomfortable, especially when you're worried about demoralizing an employee. Your first instinct might be to soften the blow or even avoid the conversation altogether. However, it's important to pause and remind yourself that feedback is essential for growth. It's often *how* feedback is delivered that can help someone grow—or shrink. Consider how to frame your feedback in a way that's both constructive and forward-looking.

When you act, focus on the issue and the path to improvement. You might say, "I've noticed some challenges here, but I'm confident we can make some improvements with a few changes. Let's talk about it." This approach helps the employee understand what needs to change while showing you're there to support them. By addressing the issue without making it personal, you keep the focus on moving forward and growing, rather than dwelling on past mistakes.

Example: A manager noticed that an employee's recent e-mails and reports contained numerous typos, which was unusual for their typically reliable work. The manager's first thought was, "I'll just fix it myself and move on. They're probably just going through something and it won't take me long." But they knew that wasn't going to help in the long run.

Instead, they met with the employee* and said, "Your writing is usually clear and professional, which I've always appreciated. I've noticed a few typos slipping into your recent work, and I wanted to check in—has something been making it harder to catch those, or is there a way I can help?"

The employee admitted they'd been rushing to meet tight deadlines and skipping their usual proofreading process. The manager acknowledged the time pressure and suggested a few quick strategies that didn't add much time, such as stepping away for a minute before rereading, using grammar tools, or printing out key documents to catch mistakes more easily.

It can be tempting as a manager to just quietly fix the mistakes yourself or avoid the conversation altogether. But when you do that, you're not just carrying the extra work—you're also missing the chance to help your employee develop and avoid repeating the same mistakes.

When People Are Rude to Those "Beneath Them" on the Org Chart

It's easy to overlook small instances of rudeness or dismissiveness, especially if you think it's out of character. However, when you pause, it's important to recognize how damaging this behavior can be to team morale and organizational culture, especially if it's happening more than you realize because it's not directed toward you, but instead at those lower on the organizational ladder.

---

* Anytime you set up a meeting with someone, consider giving context up front. Otherwise, most people's first thought is, "Am I getting fired?" even when it's something simple. For example, if you're planning to give feedback, you can say, "Hey, can we grab ten minutes later? I've got some quick feedback on the recent report." It can keep people from spiraling before you even start talking.

Consider how it feels to those on the receiving end and how it reflects on the organization, especially if your values talk about "respect" and " collaboration." Every team member is a walking billboard for your organization, even after they leave. You don't want their message to be that your organization's actions don't truly reflect its values.

When you act, address the behavior directly but privately. You might say, "I've noticed that there have been a few instances where the way you've talked to other colleagues hasn't been what we'd expect. Our values aren't just for show—it's not okay to talk to anyone that way, and certainly not someone who's on our team. Respect is important, no matter what." This reinforces that respect is a non-negotiable part of your team's culture, for everyone.

Example: A sales manager noticed that their top-performing sales employee was often quick to blame junior team members for errors—very publicly and very loudly—even when those team members weren't actually at fault. At first, the manager brushed it off, thinking it wasn't a big deal—no one had "officially" complained,* and they didn't want to risk upsetting a high performer. But after pausing to think about the bigger picture, the manager realized the behavior was taking a toll on team morale. Some team members had started skipping team meetings, and others were keeping their distance. When a new role opened up on the team—something that usually led to referrals—no one recommended a single person. That's when it clicked: Even if no one was saying it out loud, the team was feeling the impact.

The manager decided to address it privately, pulling the sales employee aside for a one-on-one. But the conversation didn't exactly go as planned. The employee pushed back immediately, saying, "Why are we even having this conversation? I'm the one hitting my numbers—maybe the newer people need to toughen up." They insisted they were just "keeping standards high" and immediately went to the head of sales, frustrated that their "behavior" was even being questioned given their performance.

---

* In an example in just a few pages, you'll learn why there's not necessarily such a thing as an "official" complaint.

It was a good reminder that these conversations don't always land the way you want, and holding people accountable for how they show up takes real buy-in across the organization. But it also reinforced why the conversation still mattered. Ignoring it would've sent a different message—that as long as you hit your numbers, how you treat people doesn't matter. These talks are rarely comfortable, but the awkwardness of one conversation is still easier than the damage to your team if you avoid it altogether.

If you're heading into a conversation like this and suspect it's not going to go smoothly, it can help to start with AI. You could ask a prompt like, *"How do I give feedback to a high performer when I don't think they'll take it well?"* You might not follow every suggestion, but running the prompt gets you thinking through different aspects: how to frame the conversation, what to say if they push back, or how to stay calm if they get defensive. Sometimes, just seeing a few options written out helps you feel more prepared to handle the conversation in real time.

And whether AI tells you to or not, it's always smart to play out the possibilities of an uncomfortable conversation ahead of time, especially what happens if they run straight to your boss. Sometimes it's worth giving your leader a heads-up before the conversation happens, so they know you're addressing the issue, why it matters, and they hear your side first.*

When You Regret How You've Acted as a Manager

It's natural—and common—to look back and realize there are moments you're not proud of as a manager, whether it's reacting out of frustration, shutting someone down too quickly, or failing to give a team member the support they need. These instances can stick in your mind with a sense of guilt, but the real opportunity is in how you respond and recover. Pausing to consider what to do in these moments shows growth, accountability, and a commitment to leading better.

---

* As a leader, remember that you might not always be getting the full story when someone brings you information. And just like you'd want your own boss to trust you enough to hear your side before jumping to conclusions, you need to do the same for your team. A simple response like, "Let me look into this," buys you time to get the facts, ask questions, and approach the situation with an open mind, especially if the first version of the story isn't the full picture.

When you act, it starts with directly owning your behavior and addressing the impact. It can be tempting to give excuses and brush it aside, but that can make it harder for the message to be heard. You might say, "I've been thinking about how I handled [specific situation], and I realize I didn't approach it in the way I should have. That wasn't fair to you, and I want to do better. I appreciate your patience, and I want to make sure I do better moving forward." This level of accountability models the behavior you want from your team and helps rebuild trust.

Example: A manager realized they had been dismissive during a team meeting when a newer employee shared an idea. In the moment, the manager was trying to get through a packed agenda and cut the employee off, because this very idea had been tried before (and had failed miserably). In the next few meetings, this employee seemed withdrawn, not saying much at all. The manager noticed how quiet they were and recognized their own mistake—the time that the employee had spoken up was one of the first team meetings they attended, and their one idea got shut down immediately. The manager meant to follow up with the employee afterward to explain why, but other things kept coming up, so they never did. As a result, the employee was left feeling embarrassed and discouraged and vowed not to share any more ideas in the future. The manager realized that while their intent wasn't to shut the employee down, the impact was clear: They had unintentionally created an environment where this employee—and probably others—would hesitate to share ideas, fearing the same reaction.

The manager decided to first follow up individually with the employee. They said, "I want to apologize for how I handled things during the meeting a few weeks ago when I cut you off when you were sharing an idea. I wish I had handled things differently back then or followed up with you right away, but I'd rather address it now than leave it unsaid. I didn't give your idea the attention it deserved, and I realize that might have left you feeling like it's not worth sharing any ideas. That's not the case. Your perspective is valuable to the team, and I'd really like to revisit your suggestion. Would you be open to discussing it?" By owning their misstep and creating an opportunity for a fresh conversation, the manager demonstrated humility and reinforced the importance of everyone's voice.

To address this with the broader team, the manager then shared in the next team meeting, "I want to make it clear that everyone's ideas matter, and I don't want to shut them down, nor do I want anyone else to. Even if we've tried something before, there may be new ways to adjust and approach it differently. Not every idea will be implemented, but I don't want anyone holding back from a great idea out of fear of feeling like it's a bad one. That's on me for not emphasizing this earlier, and I want to do better moving forward by staying more open."

The employee was surprised the manager remembered what happened in the meeting and brought it up, even if it was weeks later. They'd never had a manager do that before. It made them feel genuinely heard and respected, which boosted their confidence and made them more willing to speak up and contribute. The manager's self-awareness and effort to make things right not only rebuilt trust with the employee but also set a positive example for the team.

Mistakes don't define you as a manager—how you recover from them does. Reflecting, owning your actions, and committing to do better can transform moments of regret into opportunities to build stronger, more trusting relationships with your team.

When You Need to Motivate Your Team But You Don't Have a Budget

When you need to motivate your team but don't have the budget for raises or rewards, it's easy to feel frustrated. You may think, *How can I possibly keep people engaged without giving them more money?* And it's true that when you can't compensate employees the way you'd like (and that you know they deserve), some team members, including your best ones, might choose to leave. But it's important to pause and recognize that while raises are certainly important, there will be times that you can't offer them—the decision is out of your control. But there are always things you can control, even if the budget isn't one of them. Consider what nonmonetary incentives you can offer, such as flexibility, recognition, or professional development opportunities.

When you act, be transparent about the budget limitations but offer alternatives to support and engage your team. While money is often a strong factor in people leaving for another job, they may also realize that a higher paycheck can come with trade-offs, like longer hours or a tough work environment. You might say, "I know we can't offer raises right now, but let's talk about other ways we can help you feel supported in your role, and how we can set you up for a raise in the future. As your manager, I want to provide you with everything I can and create a work environment you enjoy and can grow in." This shows you're committed to your team's well-being, even when resources are tight. By being proactive and honest, you can offer your best approach.

Example: A manager had a team member leave for a higher-paying job elsewhere, which left the rest of the team feeling undervalued and questioning their own future at the organization. When told by leadership that raises for the remaining team members weren't possible, the manager took proactive steps to recognize and support the team in other ways. They implemented monthly recognition awards to celebrate individual contributions, offered flexible work hours, and had honest discussions about ways to recharge outside of work to achieve better work-life balance.

A few months later, the team member who had left reached out, asking if they could come back. They explained that, despite the higher pay at their new job, they hadn't felt the same level of support and enjoyment at work. The manager was happy to welcome them back, and the team member admitted that while the disappointment over compensation hadn't entirely gone away, they'd come to realize that sometimes, a higher paycheck comes with hidden costs. At their new company, there were constant expectations to work around the clock, senior "leaders" could be heard yelling at colleagues in the office, and there was little sense of job security.

The manager continued to advocate for better compensation for the team but also encouraged conversations about how a positive work environment plays a huge role in job satisfaction. This helped emphasize the importance of feeling supported, appreciated, and secure at work, something that the manager worked hard to build with their team.

When an Employee Asks for Another Raise *Too* Soon

Let's say you've recently given an employee a raise, and a few months later, they ask for another one. Your gut reaction might be, *Are they serious?* But it's important to pause and consider they may not fully understand how compensation processes work. Think about how you can use this as an opportunity to educate them about salary timelines and manage their expectations for future growth.

When you act, be both honest and empathetic. You might say, "I understand you're eager for growth, and we're excited about your contributions. However, raises are reviewed at set times to ensure fairness and consistency. Candidly, if I went to leadership and asked for another raise so soon after you just received one, their reaction might not be one you'd like. I'd rather be up front about that and give you feedback that can help you, not just in this role, but throughout your career. Let's talk about what we can do to set you up for a future raise, and when that might be most realistic." This way, you're not dismissing their request outright, but offering needed career advice and setting clear expectations for the future.

Example: A manager was caught off guard when an employee asked for another raise just a couple of months after receiving one. Instead of reacting emotionally ("Do you not remember the raise you just got two months ago?!"), the manager paused and approached the conversation calmly. They took the time to explain the company's raise cycle and performance review process, clarifying that while, yes, you can always ask, requests need to be supported by a clear explanation of what's changed since the last raise. In this case, the employee didn't have much beyond their personal belief that they deserved more. The manager reiterated, "I'm here to support you, but that includes explaining how to approach these conversations to have the best chance of success. That's not just here—that's applicable in your whole career."

The conversation helped the employee understand the timing and process better, and they appreciated the manager's honesty.

Together, they agreed to review what led to the most recent raise and identify specific steps to strengthen the case for the next one during a future regular review period. As a result, the employee left the conversation feeling grateful that their manager leveled with them and understood the type of data senior leaders would likely expect to justify another raise.

When You Have an Overwhelmed Employee

It's common to have a team member who looks like they're struggling but is hesitant to ask for help. If they're especially overwhelmed, you might feel frustrated they didn't come to you sooner. But that's where you need to pause. Consider they may not have known how to approach you or felt embarrassed to admit they had more than they could handle. Employees may fear that asking for help is a sign of weakness or incompetence.

When you act, offer your support in an open and nonjudgmental way. You could say, "I noticed you've had a lot on your plate lately. Let's talk about what's going on and how I can help." This approach not only addresses the immediate issue but also shows you're approachable and want to find ways to support them. Having these conversations early can keep the stress from becoming too much.

Example: A manager noticed that their employee looked frazzled, but assumed they could handle their workload, and if they were really having issues, they would have said something. Still, they started their next meeting by asking, "How are you doing— really doing?" The employee paused before saying they'd taken on too many projects but were afraid to speak up. They'd volunteered for some of them, so were reluctant to now admit that it was more than they'd anticipated. But it was, and it was starting to impact their entire workload.

The manager told the employee they appreciated their initiative, but also reminded them that taking on too much isn't always necessary or the best approach. They worked together to prioritize the projects, brought in help from other leaders, and set more realistic expectations to make sure the employee felt supported going forward. Their magic words for this conversation? "Thank you for raising your hand, but I'm here to tell you that you're doing enough and don't have to always take on more to prove yourself. Let's talk to other leaders and get some help for these projects, and I'll make sure to check in more regularly on workloads . . . and step in if I see you're taking on too much." Hearing those words brought a huge sense of relief to a valued employee and helped them realize the importance of only taking on work that they could deliver well and within deadlines.

When Your Team's Goals Seem Unrealistic

When senior leadership sets big goals for your team, your instinct might be to push back or say nothing and work to meet them, even if it puts stress on your team members—the very people expected to do the work to get there. Pause and acknowledge the pressure, but also recognize that managing effectively involves advocating for your team's well-being. Consider the long-term effects of trying to meet unrealistic demands—will it lead to burnout, mistakes, or high turnover? You need to frame the conversation in a way that advocates for your team while showing an understanding of leadership's goals.

Consider the best way to approach senior leadership with a goal in mind—getting the best results possible. Remember that, despite their titles, other leaders may not fully understand the realities of meeting goals, whether it's the ability to hit deadlines or the long-term effects on the team if you do manage to meet them. Instead of simply pushing back by pointing to the frustration of your team members, act by coming prepared with data and alternative solutions. Present the challenges your team is facing, but also offer realistic timelines or project adjustments that can still align with leadership's priorities. Show that you're committed to meeting goals, but in a way that is sustainable for your team.

Example: A manager was overwhelmed by constant pressure from a senior leader who kept pushing for faster project turnarounds. E-mails read, "Come on, we need this by next Friday. It's just one weekend—your team can push through!" The team, already exhausted, had been asked to work through weekends before, and it was happening more and more often. They swapped stories of family and friends who stopped making plans because they were constantly being canceled. Frustrated and ready to vent, the manager was tempted to confront the senior leader directly, and respond, "What more do you want from us?"

But instead of doing that, the manager paused and considered the bigger picture, realizing the senior leader was likely under pressure, too, and might not fully understand the toll on the team. The manager chose to have an open and candid conversation, starting with questions. They asked, "Do you know how much work this team has on their plate right now?" and calmly explained how the constant, unrealistic deadlines were leading to stress, mistakes, and burnout. The manager added that while the team *could* push to finish this project, doing so might push them over the edge—and, in this case, it wasn't truly necessary. It wasn't even a top priority for the organization.

The senior leader appreciated the transparency and admitted they hadn't realized how serious the issue had become, confirming that yes, they were also under pressure from their own leadership. Together, they escalated the concerns upward, advocating for more reasonable timelines. This conversation not only opened a productive dialogue but also equipped the manager with the data and support they needed to set clearer expectations moving forward. The senior leader recognized the importance of balancing the pressure on teams while prioritizing the most important tasks. The team felt a sense of relief—they appreciated having a leader who truly had their backs and was willing to advocate for them. The ripple effect went beyond the workplace, too, as their family and friends were finally able to make plans without assuming a last-minute work "emergency" would always come up.

When an Employee Needs an Accommodation

Whether it's a leave of absence or another type of adjustment or support, accommodations can depend on several factors, including your organization's policies and applicable laws. They can often occur for medical or religious reasons. And as a manager, it's important to remember that this doesn't just apply to employees already working for you—it can come up with candidates, too. If someone shares a need during the interview process, the goal is to listen and take it seriously, not brush it off. HR can be a key partner here to help you navigate what's fair, appropriate, and supportive.

You might not be familiar with a particular religion, medical condition, or even the reason behind a request—and that's okay. Sometimes, employees may go directly to HR with an accommodation request, and depending on the situation, HR may be legally prohibited from sharing certain details with you. That can feel frustrating, especially if you're trying to understand the full picture or wondering why the employee didn't come to you first. But keep in mind, they may have been nervous or worried about being treated differently. Instead of focusing on what you don't know, focus on what you *do* know—how the accommodation affects the work—and how you can support the employee moving forward. What matters is approaching it with respect. Ask questions thoughtfully, without judgment. Work is one of the few places in life where you may engage with people whose lives and experiences are very different from your own. Your response in these moments matters. How you show support can either build trust or shut it down.

However, sometimes you'll have to think about more than just that employee. When one employee is granted an accommodation, like a flexible work schedule, other team members may start requesting the same benefits without understanding the full context. It's easy to feel overwhelmed or defensive when dealing with multiple comments or requests, especially when they come from a lack of understanding and the fear that it's not "fair" that someone else is receiving something they aren't. The key is to pause and manage these requests or comments thoughtfully. Consider how to handle these conversations in a way that respects the privacy of the employee requesting the accommodation, while maintaining fairness within the team.

Team members may approach you with questions about why one person is receiving "special treatment." When you act, focus on educating them, while maintaining confidentiality of their colleague. Your organization may give you talking points for this, which will likely include explaining that accommodations are based on individual needs and that each situation is evaluated carefully. You might say something like, "We evaluate requests on a case-by-case basis, and what one person is eligible for might not be the same for everyone. If you have any needs or concerns, I encourage you to talk to me, and we'll see what's possible." This opens up the conversation without disclosing sensitive information.

Example: A manager had an employee who was granted a flexible work schedule due to medical reasons. Not long after, other team members noticed the change and started asking for similar flexibility, unaware that it was tied to a medical necessity. Frustrated, the manager initially wanted to explain the situation, including the specific medical condition, but paused and realized they couldn't disclose the employee's private health information—if they did, it could create a real issue.

The manager, with HR's guidance, acted thoughtfully by first asking the employee how they preferred their absences to be communicated—or if they preferred nothing be shared at all. With the employee's consent, the manager had a broader conversation with the team, explaining that workplace accommodations are evaluated on a case-by-case basis, depending on individual needs. They reassured the team that requests for flexibility would be considered fairly while also respecting everyone's privacy. By taking this approach, the manager protected the employee's confidentiality while building trust and fairness, making sure the team understood that accommodations weren't about favoritism or preferential treatment.

When a Team Member Is Afraid to Share Their Pregnancy

You may be surprised to learn how often people are afraid to share that they're pregnant. How could talking about one of the most exciting times in life feel stressful? It's often because they're afraid of how it will impact their job or even long-term career. This concern can be especially real in the United States, where, unlike many other countries, protections around pregnancy aren't always as strong or clear. As a result, employees' concerns at the start of their pregnancy often go beyond just health-related issues; they may also fear losing their job.

If a team member shares this news with you, your first instinct might be to think about how it impacts you, rather than focusing on them. You might immediately start thinking about how the team will manage their absence (especially if several team members are expecting children at the same time), but it's important to pause and recognize the courage it took for them to tell you. Think about how it would feel to take a joyful life moment and turn it into something to fear when sharing it at work. Then, consider how you can offer reassurance and create a plan that supports both the employee and the team during their absence.

When you act, respond with enthusiasm and care. You might say, "Thank you for letting me know, and congratulations! I'm here to support you. I'm so excited for you." This reassurance can be incredibly welcome after they've been carrying the worry of how their pregnancy might be received at work. And if you don't know what the leave policies are or what they're eligible for, make that clear by saying, "If you have any questions about how leave works, I can have HR reach out to you to make sure you have all the information you need." This way, you're relying on the function that handles it, and the team member isn't surprised by someone reaching out.

Example: When an employee told her manager she was pregnant, the manager was shocked. They wondered, *We just named her the head of the new store opening—how could she have hidden this from us?* The employee confided that she hadn't spoken up earlier because she was afraid it would cost her the promotion and hurt her career long term. The employee even offered to shorten her maternity leave or stay connected by e-mail to make sure the opening went smoothly. The manager felt terrible that this employee, who had just shared big life news, was offering to sacrifice precious time with her newborn just to make sure the store opening went smoothly. The manager reached out to HR, and they shared that other stores had successfully opened while managers were on parental leave, with teams collaborating to ensure coverage. The manager reached out to other leaders to get their best practices, and also connected the employee with managers so she could learn from their experiences.

In the end, the employee took her full leave and the store opening went smoothly, thanks in part to cross-training additional managers (which not only helped ensure coverage during her absence but also created development opportunities for others). The manager understood why the employee had kept her pregnancy quiet, but didn't want anyone else to feel like they had to do the same. With the manager's encouragement, HR organized lunch-and-learn webinars where team members and leaders shared their experiences of balancing personal needs with career growth, offering valuable lessons and support for others in similar situations.

When a Team Member Suffers a Personal Loss or Challenge

One of the toughest moments as a manager is when a team member experiences personal difficulty, including the loss of a loved one. You might find yourself juggling how to support them while still ensuring the team meets its goals or deadlines. It can feel like you have to push empathy aside to keep work on track. However, this is the time to pause and recognize how much your team member needs support as a person, not just as an employee. Consider how challenging it can be to focus on work while grieving, and think about the kind of support they need at this moment. Remember, you don't have to take on their grief, but it's important to acknowledge its impact. When someone is dealing with personal loss, it will naturally affect their performance.

When you act, prioritize empathy while figuring out how to keep things running smoothly. You might say, "I'm really sorry for your loss. I can find out everything you're eligible for and we can make sure things are covered while you're out." In moments like this, reaching out to HR on their behalf can be a welcome step. This is when your leadership matters most—showing understanding and flexibility to the employee while coordinating with HR for resources and communicating with other stakeholders about potential delays. Taking these actions not only supports the team member during a difficult time but also builds trust within your team, who see you as a leader who genuinely cares about their well-being.

Example: A manager felt devastated when a key employee lost a family member just before a major product launch. They knew how close the team member was to their family, but the manager also felt overcome with guilt, because their first thought was, *How will this impact the deadlines?* The manager took a moment to pause and consider what the employee must be going through. Understanding the significance of the launch, the employee offered to attend only part of the funeral to still be there for the team. However, the manager recognized how unfair and unreasonable that request was and insisted they attend the entire service and be with their family. "Focus on your family. We'll figure it out," the manager said.

Instead, the manager gathered the team to discuss what could realistically be achieved and then communicated the situation to senior leadership. The team came together, stepping up to take on key project responsibilities so their colleague could have the space to grieve. While it wasn't an easy process, the project *was* completed successfully, and the team grew closer through their support for one another. Acknowledging their hard work, the manager pushed for spot performance bonuses for the entire team. Additionally, they held follow-up meetings to explore processes that would allow the team to better support each other on short notice, regardless of the reason.

When Someone Makes Inappropriate Jokes in the Workplace

When someone on your team makes an inappropriate comment they think is "just a joke," it's easy to want to brush it off or hope no one else caught it. But pause and think about the impact these comments can have on your team's culture. Consider how the "joke" can make team members uncomfortable and hurt morale. When you don't take action, even if no one asks you to, it can send a message about your leadership. Your responsibility is to your team, and to make sure that the workplace is inclusive and respectful, even when it means having tough conversations.

When you act, it's important to address the situation promptly. If the comment or joke may violate organizational policy, you should reach out to HR privately to determine the appropriate next steps. For more general comments, you might say, "I wanted to talk with you one-on-one about something I heard. That comment wasn't appropriate, especially in a workplace setting. Being respectful means making sure we don't make others feel uncomfortable." This approach addresses the behavior directly while reinforcing expectations for professionalism and respect in the workplace.

And don't forget to be mindful of your own words, too. As a manager, what you say carries weight—sometimes more than you realize. A joke that feels harmless to you might land very differently for someone else, especially if it touches on their work performance, appearance, or personal situations. Even offhand remarks can make someone feel excluded or self-conscious. Being thoughtful about your timing, tone, and language helps reinforce a culture where everyone feels respected and works together as a team.

Example: A manager once overheard an employee making fun of a job candidate they had just interviewed, ridiculing the college the candidate had attended. Initially, the manager thought it was harmless since the candidate wasn't going to get an offer, and the joke didn't touch on "sensitive topics" like age or gender. But after considering the broader impact on the team's culture, they spoke privately with the employee, explaining why the joke wasn't appropriate—that not every candidate will be a good fit, but it doesn't reflect well on the team to make jokes at their expense. Making fun of where someone went to school made the team member seem rude and inconsiderate in a company where two of the core values were "professionalism" and "respect."

At first, the employee was defensive. They shrugged it off, saying it was "not a big deal" and "no one was supposed to hear it anyway." When the manager brought up the company's values—like professionalism and respect—the employee actually laughed and said, "Company values?! Are you serious?"

But the manager stuck with it. They explained, "I get it, sometimes those words feel like they're just printed on a poster. But they matter. They're how we show up—and that includes how we talk about people, even the ones who don't end up working here."

The employee paused, still clearly not loving the conversation, but eventually admitted they hadn't really thought about how those offhand comments could shape how the team shows up. They agreed to be more mindful going forward.

By addressing it, the manager didn't just shut down a careless joke. They made it clear the team's values aren't just words on a page—they're how the team works, speaks, and represents the organization, inside and outside the building.

When an Employee Asks You "Not to Tell Anyone"

If an employee asks you to keep something "confidential," it's important to pause and consider carefully about what they're about to share—before making any promises. It's natural to want to support the employee and honor their request, but there are situations where confidentiality isn't an option. Legal concerns, safety risks, or issues that could impact others on the team may require you to take action.

It's also a good reminder that there isn't always such a thing as an "official" complaint. Sometimes just telling a manager—whether the employee meant it that way or not—is enough to trigger the organization's responsibility to look into the situation. You can't always sit on information just because someone frames it as "just between us."

When you act, be up front with the employee about what you can and can't keep confidential. You might say: "I appreciate you trusting me with this, and I want to respect your privacy as much as I can. That said, depending on what you share, there may be things I'm required to follow up on or escalate, especially if it affects others or the organization overall. But we also have nonretaliation policies for a reason. Let me think about what's needed, and I'll follow up with you on next steps." This gives you time to connect with HR (or whoever handles these situations at your organization) to understand next steps. If HR is going to take the lead, it's helpful to ask whether you can give the employee a heads-up before they hear from someone else so they're not caught off guard.

Being up front shows the employee you respect their trust but also reminds them that part of your role is supporting them while still following through on your responsibilities as a leader in the organization.

Example: A manager had an employee confide in them about something they witnessed at a work retreat that made them "uncomfortable." The employee was hesitant to share more details, saying they didn't want to "start a rumor or cause unnecessary drama." The manager paused and explained that certain matters, especially those that could impact the well-being or safety of others, need to be looked into for a reason. They reassured the employee that reporting doesn't automatically mean jumping to conclusions, but rather ensuring that concerns are looked into and addressed appropriately. After discussing the situation, the employee agreed to share the details, and the manager explained that HR would look into the matter to ensure it was handled properly and the team member felt supported. This approach reassured the employee that their concerns were being taken seriously, while also helping them understand the importance of addressing the issue in the right way.

When an Employee Makes a Complaint About You

When it comes to employee complaints, sometimes the issue might involve you, whether it comes from your team member or someone else. When an employee raises a concern about you, your first reaction might be defensiveness or frustration. But pause and recognize that even though it's uncomfortable, feedback is valuable and can provide insight into how others perceive your leadership. Consider what may have led to this complaint—was it a communication issue or perhaps a complete misunderstanding? Listening with an open mind can help you understand the employee's perspective and what's truly going on.

When you act, approach the situation with openness rather than defensiveness. An employee might share feedback or concerns with you directly. If that happens, keep in mind that it can show a significant amount of trust for your team member to bring it up to you. You might say, "Thank you for sharing this with me. I'm sure it wasn't easy, and I'd like to talk through it so we can work toward a solution together." This response shows maturity and a willingness to improve, which helps build respect from both the employee and the rest of the team.

Employees have different ways they can raise concerns, and while it's often ideal for them to bring issues directly to you, that's not always how it happens. They may not feel comfortable, or they might worry about how it'll be received. If you learn about a concern through someone else or by accident, it can make things more complicated—for you and for them. That's why it's so important to create an environment where people know they won't be punished for speaking up. Your HR team will likely guide you on how to handle this in a fair and supportive way. That goes beyond just avoiding phrases like "Why didn't you tell me?" It also means being mindful not to retaliate in subtle ways, like excluding someone from meetings, taking away responsibilities, or giving harsher feedback just because they spoke up. In fact, in the United States, retaliation is the most common type of claim filed with the Equal Employment Opportunity Commission,[1] the federal agency responsible for handling workplace complaints. It's not just something that feels unfair; it can carry real consequences.

That's why it's crucial to handle these situations with care, making sure the employee doesn't feel singled out or uncomfortable for having shared their perspective. If the concern comes through HR, take the time to understand what's expected of you and approach it with seriousness and openness. And if the issue surfaces more informally—say, you hear that someone on your team has been venting or seems frustrated—you don't have to ignore it or get defensive. Instead, take a proactive, human approach by checking in privately and inviting an honest conversation. You might say, "I get the sense that you're feeling frustrated with work. I might be off base, but I wanted to check in and see how you're really feeling. Your perspective is important to me, and I'd like to know whether there's anything I can do differently." That kind of outreach doesn't just show you care; it shows that your team can trust you, even when it's hard.

This kind of response invites a more open conversation and shows that you're committed to improving without making the employee feel singled out. It's equally important to ensure the employee doesn't feel targeted for sharing their thoughts. That's an important point to remember, because it's much easier to say you want feedback than to actually hear it and consider how to act on it. Reinforce, when appropriate, that their concerns are valued and seen as an opportunity to strengthen your working relationship and not something that will be held against them. By keeping the conversation constructive and focused on solutions, you show that you take the feedback seriously and are committed to building a healthy, trusting culture where team members feel comfortable bringing up their thoughts (and even concerns) in the future.

Example: When a manager was covering e-mails for an employee on leave, they were shocked to discover e-mails making fun of them. The manager's first instinct was to fire the employee for insubordination—after all, making comments like that about a manager crosses a line. But after taking a moment to pause and reflect, the manager considered the underlying messages in the jokes, and realized they'd been unintentionally micromanaging the team. What initially felt like a personal attack started to look more like frustration bubbling over. Rather than punishing the employee, the manager decided to turn it into a teaching moment—for everyone—opening up a conversation about trust, autonomy, and how to work better together moving forward.

When the employee returned, the manager acted, bringing up the e-mails and explaining that, while hurt, they wanted to use the situation as a learning opportunity. The employee was mortified and apologized for what they'd said. The manager acknowledged that giving "upward" feedback isn't easy, but emphasized that it would be more constructive if that feedback were shared directly, rather than just discussed among the team. By addressing the situation openly and talking about how to rebuild trust, the manager turned a difficult moment into a chance for growth, ultimately strengthening their relationship with both the employee and the team.

When You Have Conflict Within Your Team

Dealing with conflict between team members can be draining, and your first thought might be, *Please grow up. I don't have time for this.* But it's important to pause and recognize that unresolved conflict often grows into bigger problems. Consider how the issue is affecting team morale, productivity, and relationships. The first step is determining whether it's a minor disagreement that can be worked out internally or a more serious conflict that might require HR or another neutral party's involvement. Minor conflicts can usually be handled directly, while more serious issues—especially those involving inappropriate behavior—may need to be escalated.

When you act, start by gauging the severity of the conflict. If it's a minor disagreement, facilitating a conversation between the parties might be all that's needed to clear the air. You could say, "It seems like there's some tension between you two. Let's talk through it so we can find a way to move forward." This approach can help resolve the conflict before it spirals, and shows your team that you're committed to maintaining a healthy work environment. However, in cases of more serious conflict, don't hesitate to involve HR. For example, if the issue involves allegations of discrimination, bullying, or a breach of organizational policy, the situation should be handled carefully, following organizational procedures to ensure fairness and legality.

Even when you deal with a relatively minor conflict, it's important to make sure it doesn't escalate or linger, even after it's resolved. As a manager, you can use your leadership to help team members understand how to actually move forward rather than letting negative feelings remain. How can you do that? My favorite tip comes from a potentially unexpected source. During a team training session on conflict resolution, an employee shared a quote from singer Jelly Roll that stuck with me: "There's a reason the windshield is bigger than the rearview mirror."[2]

This simple idea encourages focusing on the future rather than dwelling on the past. And it resonates with every leader and team member I've mentioned it to since. Whether the conflict is small or significant, adopting this mindset helps the team take a forward-looking approach, reset relationships, and work together in a more productive, solution-oriented way.

Example: A manager noticed ongoing tension between two team members. It started with "small" behaviors—eye-rolling, sarcastic responses to each other's ideas, and always staying as far as possible from each other during meetings. Eventually, one team member announced, "I don't trust them, and I'm definitely not meeting with them. If they want something, they can e-mail me." Initially, the manager hoped the conflict would resolve on its own, but when it became the main topic of conversation among the team, they decided to step in.

The manager brought the two employees together for an informal conversation, framing it as a chance to "clear the air." It turned out that the whole thing started with a misunderstanding, that one team member thought a colleague had taken credit for their work, when that wasn't the case at all. They only realized what really happened when they actually sat down and talked about it. The manager got the team members to see that asking questions and not assuming the worst were important steps in preventing misunderstandings. They also took the opportunity to explain what had happened to the entire team, assuring everyone that they would reach out directly if something like this came up again (though, fortunately, it never did).

In a separate situation, where an employee reported feeling "harassed," the manager recognized the seriousness of the issue and immediately reached out to HR. They reassured the employee that HR would conduct a fair investigation and follow up with clear next steps. Understanding the importance of handling this appropriately, the manager then let HR take the lead and asked for guidance on how to proceed, both with the employee involved and with the rest of the team. The manager also asked HR how to address any potential questions from other team members, ensuring the situation was handled with care and professionalism.

By addressing each situation based on its severity—managing minor conflicts with proactive conversations and escalating serious concerns appropriately—the manager approached both issues effectively. Ensuring that team members know what to expect in each situation is key to maintaining consistency, building trust, and making employees feel comfortable coming to you when issues arise.

When Buzzwords Become Trendy on Social Media

When phrases like "quiet quitting" start making the rounds, it's easy to roll your eyes and write them off as another trendy excuse to not work. A lot of managers do. But usually, these buzzwords reflect something deeper—burnout, frustration, or feeling like the extra effort isn't being recognized.

The tricky part? You're probably not going to walk up and say, "Hey, are you quiet quitting?" If that would feel awkward for you, it would likely feel 10 times more for your team member. But you can use these trends as an opportunity to check in. AI can help with that. You might throw in a prompt like: *"How can I bring up quiet quitting in a way that helps my team open up, without making it uncomfortable?"*

Example: A manager kept seeing "quiet quitting" pop up in articles and on social media and started wondering whether anyone on their team was feeling that way. They asked AI for ideas, got a few suggestions, and one stood out: Be direct (but not accusatory), be real, and actually connect it to how people may be feeling.

In their next team meeting, the manager said: "I've seen this quiet quitting thing everywhere, and it made me think about how you all are actually feeling about your work. I don't want anyone here to feel like you can't be honest if you're ever feeling frustrated or stuck. I wanted to have an honest conversation about workload—what's working, what's not, and where I can be real about what we can try and what we can't."

The team laughed when the manager brought it up. Some admitted that when they first heard the buzzword mentioned, they thought they were about to get called out or get in trouble. But they appreciated that it turned into a real conversation. A few employees shared that they were feeling stretched thin, but they also offered ideas for how the team could work smarter and feel more motivated. The manager said, "This isn't a one-time, check-the-box conversation. Sometimes it takes seeing something outside of work to remind me I need to check in and make sure we're actually talking about this."

When an Employee Expresses Interest in Interviewing for Another Team

When an employee tells you they're interested in a role on another team, your first reaction might be, "But you can't leave me. I need you!" Pause and remember that supporting their growth—whether it's on your team or another—is part of your role as a manager. Consider how to approach this situation in a way that encourages the employee's development without making them feel guilty or discouraged.

When you act, have an open and supportive conversation. You could say, "I hear you're interested in a new opportunity, and while we'd miss having you on this team, I want to support you in pursuing your career goals. Let's talk about how I can help you with this process." This shows that you're invested in their growth, and even if they move to another team, they will appreciate the support and leave on positive terms.

Example: A manager was initially in shock when one of their best employees mentioned wanting to interview for another team. The manager immediately assumed the employee was unhappy with their role or that it had something to do with their personal feelings toward them. However, after pausing to talk with them, they learned that the team member simply wanted to explore a different area to gain new experience. Understanding this, the manager supported the employee's decision and offered to help with the process. This not only helped maintain a positive, professional relationship but also showed the employee that the manager valued their growth. In the end, the employee appreciated the manager's support so much that they helped identify a replacement for their own role, and they went on to recommend the manager as a mentor to others.

When Your Best Employee Quits

When a top performer gives notice, it can feel like a huge setback. Your initial instinct might be panic ("How are we going to get things done? Is everyone else going to quit now, too?!"), but pause and remember that people leave jobs for all kinds of reasons, not just dissatisfaction with you. Consider how their departure will impact the team and what steps you can take to manage the transition smoothly, including for the rest of the team that's remaining.

When you act, show support and gratitude for their contributions while also focusing on the team's needs. You could say, "We're sad to see you go, but we're excited about your next step. Let's work together to ensure a smooth transition." This type of response leaves the door open for future collaboration and reassures your team that you can handle the change with grace. Internally, there may be other considerations to address—such as if the employee is leaving for a competitor—but prioritizing a respectful and seamless departure is often far more valuable than any initial frustration or instinct to react.

Example: A manager was caught off guard and upset when their top-performing employee unexpectedly resigned. Initially, they assumed the worst—that the employee was unhappy with the work, the team, or even the manager's leadership. Instead of reacting emotionally, though, the manager paused and had a candid conversation to understand the situation. The employee explained that they had received an offer from another company that would double their salary at a time when their family really needed the money. They admitted they had been nervous about sharing the news, fearing they might be asked to leave right away.

Rather than expressing disappointment or frustration, the manager chose to support the employee's decision and focus on ensuring a smooth transition. They worked together to wrap up key projects, redistribute responsibilities, and celebrate the employee's contributions to the team. The respectful and thoughtful way the manager handled the situation not only earned the departing employee's appreciation but also strengthened the trust of the remaining team members, who respected the manager's professionalism and care. Even after leaving, the employee continued to speak highly of the manager and their experience, proving how good leadership during transitions can have ripple effects that last long after someone leaves.

WHY IT'S IMPORTANT TO HAVE THE HARD CONVERSATIONS

Difficult situations in management can take many forms, whether it's addressing performance issues, mediating between team members, or navigating personal challenges with employees. These moments are often uncomfortable, but they're also where your true leadership is formed. It's easy to get caught up in the stress, but it's critical to pause and think about the situation from your team member's perspective. What might seem like a minor issue to you could feel overwhelming or deeply personal to them. Showing you understand this and are willing to approach the situation with empathy can transform a difficult conversation into an opportunity for connection.

Consider that these challenging moments are often when employees are most vulnerable. Whether they're coming to you with a personal issue, giving or getting critical feedback, or seeking guidance, they're looking to see how you'll respond. Will you react with frustration or dismissiveness, or will you take the time to listen and offer support? Leadership isn't about having all the answers or fixing every problem on the spot; it's about being present, showing care, and creating an environment where team members feel heard and valued. When you lead with compassion, even in difficult conversations, you're reinforcing a culture of trust and mutual respect.

Act with the knowledge that, even though these situations can be uncomfortable, they're actually the building blocks of a strong team. Your ability to have tough conversations, and do it with poise and empathy, shapes the trust and loyalty your team has in you. Leadership isn't always about making big decisions; it's often about showing care and compassion in small but meaningful ways. When you handle difficult conversations with grace, you create an environment where your team feels safe to voice their concerns, knowing you'll respond with understanding and support. Those little moments go a long way in strengthening relationships and building a resilient, high-performing team.

At the end of the day, the technical skills that got you your role are just one piece of the puzzle. It's your people skills—how you connect, empathize, and lead through tough situations—that will truly determine your success as a manager. By remembering and applying the **Pause-Consider-Act** framework, no matter what situations you're facing, you give yourself the space to respond thoughtfully rather than react impulsively, allowing you to build trust, encourage open communication, and ultimately create a more cohesive and resilient team.

BE READY FOR DIFFICULT CONVERSATIONS

If you haven't already, set up that meeting with HR to talk through how to handle the tough situations and what you need to be aware of as a manager. It's your chance to make sure you understand what's yours to manage (and what support and resources you have) and when you need to loop in HR or other teams so they can take more control.

I've seen managers try to deal with things solo that they probably shouldn't have, and I've had those "wish we'd talked sooner" moments, usually sitting in a conference room with me as HR . . . or worse, me as the lawyer.

I've also had those conversations where leaders shared more with me about what's really happening with their teams, and it made my support as HR a whole lot better. Personally, my time working in sales before law school made me much more effective working with sales teams as HR, because I've lived that world. But not everyone in HR has that experience. You bringing them into the reality of what your team is dealing with—the pressure, the personalities, the messy parts—can help them give support that's actually realistic and helpful, not just policy on paper.

HR can help you spot when a minor issue might escalate or when something needs to be documented or handled formally. But they can only support you well if they understand your world. Those up-front conversations make it easier to navigate the gray areas and avoid scrambling later when something comes up.

During these conversations, it can be helpful to ask for their practical advice on managing difficult conversations, taking the principles in this book and applying them to your specific team and organization. This can also be a good time to suggest setting up an open forum where managers can discuss common challenges. The goal isn't to gossip about specific employees, but to create a space for managers to share examples and tips that have worked for them. Internal manager peer groups or cohort sessions can offer a chance to talk through tough situations, seek advice, and collaborate on solutions. Not only does this boost each manager's confidence, but it also helps spread practical best practices throughout the leadership team.

By making these conversations with HR and other managers a regular part of your leadership development, you'll build a stronger support system and expand your toolkit for handling the "people" challenges that will come your way. Whether it's learning how to approach a delicate performance issue or finding out what has worked for others in situations like a team member's personal struggles, these discussions can provide a well-rounded perspective. It also helps keep things consistent across the organization, so managers are on the same page when it comes to handling tough conversations and challenges. This way, employees across different teams get treated fairly and with empathy.

In addition to talking with HR, think about reaching out to your own leader or other leaders you respect to learn how they handle tough situations. These conversations can provide you with real-world examples and insight into how experienced managers handle the challenges you're facing. Ask them about the resources they rely on, the guidance they've received, and the strategies they've found most effective. This could be anything from specific communication techniques, to how they make decisions, to how they've learned to balance empathy with accountability when leading their teams.

By having these conversations with leaders you respect, you'll gain invaluable wisdom on how to manage people more effectively, especially when dealing with tough situations like those we've covered in this book. You might also find that these leaders use certain tools—like management books, online resources, or mentorship networks—that could be helpful for you to explore. Furthermore, understanding how they figure out what to do when they don't have all the answers can serve as a reminder that even the most successful leaders continue to learn and adapt.

These discussions can also strengthen your relationship with your leader, as they'll see your commitment to improving your management skills. By asking for their advice, you're not just showing good initiative; you're also showing that you value their experience and want to learn from it. These quick conversations can create a solid support network of HR, other managers, and senior leaders, giving you real people to lean on when actual situations come up.

Questions for Self-Reflection

- **How do I usually react when a tough conversation comes up?**

  Take a moment to reflect on how you usually feel and respond in challenging situations. Do you react right away, or do you pause and think it through first?

- **When I'm faced with a problem, how would others describe my response?**

  Consider whether you're taking the time to truly understand your team's point of view before reacting. Are you open to listening, or do you immediately focus on solving the issue?

- **How do I keep my emotions in check when managing tricky people issues?**

  Think about how you handle stress in the moment. Are you giving yourself time to pause and reflect, or do you let emotions drive your decisions?

- **Am I balancing solving today's problems with building the team for tomorrow?**

  Think about whether you're just putting out fires or whether you're also focusing on your team's long-term growth. How are you helping them grow beyond just dealing with the immediate challenges?

- **Is there a difficult situation I wish I'd handled differently?**

  Reflect on a time when a conversation or conflict didn't go as planned. What could you have done differently, what can you do about it now, and what lessons can you take from it moving forward?

Chapter 10

Thinking Strategically

Seeing the Big Picture
(and Making It Happen)

I've lost track of how many mornings I've started with a to-do list I was sure I'd power through only to have the day completely derailed by e-mails, meetings, last-minute asks, and surprise issues. By mid-morning, that tidy list is buried under a pile of new things I didn't see coming. And by the end of the day? I'm staring at those same untouched tasks, wondering whether I should just change the date and try again tomorrow. It's a familiar loop for a lot of managers;* we're stuck in constant reaction mode, dealing with the urgent instead of carving out space to lead and plan intentionally.

As a manager, it's incredibly easy to get wrapped up in "what I need to get done right now." When your day is consumed by new challenges, it can feel like you're just trying to stay afloat. But thinking strategically means pulling back from that immediate pressure and learning to manage what feels like chaos. It's about looking beyond the day-to-day crises (or even questions or unexpected situations that feel overwhelming) and setting yourself—and your team—up for long-term success. It's making time investments now that you're grateful for in the future. This shift requires not only

---

* And me too—just like I shared at the beginning of Chapter 7, with that one-month project deadline.

managing tasks but also stepping into your leadership role and focusing on how your team can think beyond just today. Recognizing this shift in perspective is crucial, especially if you've recently been promoted from an individual contributor role. Your job is no longer about handling everything yourself; it's about making choices to help your team succeed, including thinking strategically about the short term and the long term.

LETTING GO OF WHAT YOU NEED TO LET GO

One of the most important aspects of strategic thinking as a manager is learning how to let go of (certain) details. You might have spent years mastering your previous role, knowing every intricate detail of how things should be done. You might have a lot of opinions on how everyone else should do it, too. But as a manager, your role changes—it's no longer about knowing every detail, but about setting up your team to handle those details while you focus on the bigger picture. Trying to stay involved in every small task will pull you away from the more strategic aspects of your role, which should involve thinking about where the team is heading, how to motivate others, and what your long-term goals are. Shifting from the mindset of an individual contributor can be tough, but if you don't make that change (and leverage available technology to help make it happen more efficiently), you'll likely end up feeling overwhelmed and struggle to lead effectively.

So, how do you stay on top of the work today, while also thinking ahead for tomorrow? Start by pausing and evaluating how you're communicating with your team. Are you focused on providing the support they need to do their jobs without constantly checking in? One simple change you can make is to have regular one-on-one meetings where you discuss progress and set expectations for the week. I mentioned earlier in this book how important these meetings are. A lot of managers assume that as they climb the organizational ladder, their role becomes less hands-on, thinking, *We're all busy—I don't have time for one-on-ones!* But for effective strategic leadership, these meetings are even more crucial. They give you dedicated time to connect with team members, understand their needs, and offer support, without micromanaging or hovering.

Also, think about setting aside those specific office hours where your team can come to you with urgent questions, even beyond your one-on-ones. If you're in the office, you can be physically present for meetings, but if you're traveling or working remotely, you can block off time on your calendar to be available for conversations. This gives your team a dedicated time to reach out when they need support, while allowing you to schedule other uninterrupted time for focused work. It creates a structured way for your team to get help without interrupting your ability to think and plan strategically.

Consider how you're communicating with your team, especially when passing along information you learn from others. Part of leadership is recognizing that you don't need to share everything with your team. It's not about hiding information, but rather understanding that they might not be ready to handle all the details right away, especially when things are still uncertain. By focusing on proactive solutions instead of fueling fear, you'll help keep your team aligned with the company's goals and create a calmer, more productive environment. For example, if upper management hints that cuts might be coming or that more efficiency is needed, how you present this matters. Telling your team, "We might need to cut twenty percent of the team and raise revenue by thirty percent" without a plan will just cause panic, not productivity. Instead, frame it like this: "We know that it's a tough time in our industry, but let's focus on what we can control and try as a team. What ideas do you have to help us be more efficient and make a positive impact before we're asked to?"

And if you're not sure what to avoid saying—or where you might accidentally step into something you shouldn't—you can always use an AI prompt like: *"What common traps should I watch out for as a leader on a [insert function] team, especially if I want to get the work done without trying to do it all myself, or oversharing things my team doesn't need to know?"*

Act by creating a more intentional structure around your time and your team's time. Block out time in your calendar, not just for meetings but also for strategic planning, reviewing team goals, and seeking out development opportunities for your team. For example, if development is important to you, does your calendar reflect that? Do you have dedicated time for mentoring or training? Plan sessions where you and your team share best practices, review the work together, and focus on long-term goals rather than daily tasks. When you actively carve out time for strategic work, you set the example for your team to do the same, moving away from reactionary habits and toward thoughtful, intentional action.

Example: A sales manager sensed growing concern from senior leadership about declining revenues and knew the team needed to be ready for potential challenges. Instead of waiting for the challenges to actually happen, the manager took a proactive approach. They scheduled a team meeting to create a playbook focused on improving efficiency and driving results.

To kick off the process, the manager used AI to help structure their approach. They asked a prompt of: *"What steps can I take with my sales team to improve efficiency and results without overwhelming them?"* The responses sparked a plan to map out each step of the team's work, address common bottlenecks, and figure out which tasks were actually driving the most revenue.

The manager also kept the conversation approachable. Instead of calling it "best practices," they asked the team, "What are things you do that help you work better, even if you never thought they were important enough to share with the team?" That question uncovered simple but effective habits team members had never brought up, largely because they seemed too "basic" to mention.

The manager used AI again to help organize those insights into a practical, clear playbook. It included guidelines for streamlining communication, strategies for closing deals, and tools to save time and stay focused.

So when senior leadership eventually announced tighter targets, the team was ready. They leaned on the playbook to stay aligned, implement proven strategies, and maintain a sense of control and direction. By anticipating concerns, tapping into both the team's experience and AI as a resource, the manager helped the team navigate uncertainty and demonstrate that they could deliver results under pressure.

REGAINING CONTROL OF YOUR TIME

Mastering time management often starts with the exercise I mentioned earlier—taking a moment to reflect on how you're currently using your time. It's easy to fall into a reactive pattern, always tackling the next issue or task that comes up. But to be a truly strategic leader, you need to break that cycle by setting aside time to focus on the bigger picture. In the act phase, take a hard look at your calendar and how your meetings are structured. If you realize you should be spending more time developing your team, think about how you can make that happen. It doesn't always mean adding more meetings; sometimes, it's about looking at existing opportunities and seeing whether you can involve your team in those. The key is to use a tool you likely rely on every day—your calendar—and make sure it reflects your priorities and goals.

When I talked about one-on-one meetings with team members, did you think (or rethink) about yours strategically? Are you providing valuable feedback, or are they becoming routine check-ins with little depth? Taking the time to rethink these conversations can create much more meaningful opportunities for growth. For example, if your usual process is to assign a task to a team member, have them complete it, and then give feedback afterward, why not shorten the process? Use your one-on-one time—or set aside time—to screen share while they're working through the task. You could even make it a team activity, with everyone collaborating on something together. Be sure to emphasize that the goal is to share how each person approaches their work and highlight best practices. Providing real-time coaching while a team member works through a task makes feedback more immediate and actionable. Not only does this make better use of your time, but it also helps your team get work done more efficiently and effectively, while helping them learn from each other.

Take, for example, a manager who felt constantly buried under back-to-back meetings and endless e-mail follow-ups. They were so caught up in the day-to-day that they couldn't find time to focus on long-term planning, which was starting to hold the team back. Realizing this, the manager made a change: They began blocking out two-hour windows twice a week for focused work, and they stuck to it. During this time, they tackled big-picture priorities, such as setting team goals, creating career development plans, and ensuring projects aligned with the company's vision.

They also revamped their one-on-ones, adding a coaching component to discuss in-progress work and offer real-time guidance. This shift made their feedback more meaningful and gave team members the support they needed to grow. The result? A more engaged, motivated team that felt they were not only contributing to the company's success but also advancing in their own careers.

Becoming a manager doesn't mean you automatically get more hours in the day or can handle everything on your own. It's still crucial to stay in the loop with the same information your team has, understanding the priorities and deadlines you're all working toward. While you can't always control everything, by managing what you can and ensuring your calendar aligns with your priorities, you're not just ticking off tasks. You're choosing to lead with intention and strategy, where small time investments now can pay off significantly in the future.

BEING (REALISTICALLY) AVAILABLE

Another part of thinking strategically is clear, *realistic* communication with your team. In Chapter 5, I talked about the trap of open-door policies, and in Chapter 6, how delegating well is key to doing the work that actually needs you (and giving up what others can do and learn to do). This chapter is where those lessons meet real life. It's not enough to know the theory—you have to put it into practice.

That means being intentional with your time by creating space for your team while also being clear about where you need to step back. If you're always available to everyone, your own priorities won't get the attention they deserve. And if you're holding on to tasks that could be handled by others, you're not leading strategically—you're reacting. Stepping back isn't about doing less; it's about making space to do what matters most. I'll use an example that weaves lessons from those earlier chapters and brings them to life.

Example: A manager found themselves constantly bombarded with minor questions throughout the day—door knocks, "Have a minute?" messages, Teams pings—making it nearly impossible to stay focused on anything. After pausing to reflect, they realized their well-intentioned open-door policy was actually getting in the way of being an effective leader. So, they made three key changes:

1. First, they set up specific one-on-one meetings and office hours, making it clear when team members would have their full attention.

2. Second, they looked at what they were still holding on to that someone else could own and began delegating those tasks more thoughtfully.

3. And third, they started using some of that designated time to offer broader guidance—like how to approach tough decisions or handle tricky situations—so their team felt more confident and equipped. They even created clear guidelines for common scenarios, helping team members take action on their own without second-guessing themselves.

As a result, team members felt more supported, not less, because they knew when they'd have time set aside with their manager and they felt trusted to handle more on their own. The manager regained control of their time, shifted from constant reaction mode to strategic planning, and saw their team become more confident and empowered in the process.

THINKING BEYOND YOUR OWN TEAM

As a manager, it's essential to think beyond your own department and build relationships with other leaders across the organization. Transitioning from simply defending your team's interests to advocating for them in a way that also recognizes the broader company goals is a key part of strategic thinking. When you take the time to understand how different functions operate, it not only builds goodwill but also helps you make more informed decisions that benefit the entire organization. Rather than focusing solely on your team's needs, learn how to position your team's contributions in a way that aligns with other departments' priorities, building a sense of collaboration and shared success.

One way to strengthen these relationships is by regularly meeting with leaders from other departments. Set up informal coffee chats or brief one-on-one meetings to ask questions, such as "What's your team working on right now?" or "What are your goals this quarter?" These conversations can help you understand their challenges, their successes, and how your teams might work together more effectively. A great follow-up question could be, "What do you wish other departments knew about your team and the work you're doing?" This can open up a more in-depth dialogue and uncover potential areas for collaboration or support that weren't previously on your radar.

Building these connections also gives you a chance to advocate for your own team in a more informed and strategic way. When you understand the bigger picture, you're better positioned to speak on your team's behalf, showing how your work contributes to the overall goals of the organization. This proactive approach helps you move from simply protecting your team to elevating their impact across the organization. By thinking beyond your immediate department, you help build stronger, more collaborative relationships that benefit not just your team but the entire company.

Example: Two departments—sales and information security—were frequently at odds, clashing over deadlines and expectations. The sales team prioritized booking deals and driving revenue, while the information security team focused on conducting thorough reviews to protect the company's data and risk management. The tension mounted because sales wanted to move quickly, while security's reviews took time, leading both teams to focus more on their frustrations with each other than on solving the problem. Productivity dipped, blame was rampant, and the friction between the teams was hard to ignore.

Realizing the situation couldn't continue, the sales manager took a strategic step to address the conflict. Instead of letting the frustration linger, they reached out to the information security manager for a one-on-one conversation to better understand their goals, challenges, and the root cause of the delays. This open discussion helped build trust between the two leaders and laid the foundation for finding a workable solution.

After gaining a better understanding of each side's priorities and concerns, the managers arranged a joint meeting with both teams. To kick things off, team members from each side introduced themselves and shared their current projects and responsibilities. This helped both teams remember that there were actually human beings behind the e-mail addresses and gain a better understanding of the daily pressures their colleagues were facing. Next, employees from both teams who had recently worked together on a project were invited to share their experiences. They shared the challenges they encountered, how they overcame them, and what they learned from having open, productive conversations instead of falling into an "us versus them" mentality. It gave everyone a real-life example of how collaboration, instead of finger-pointing, can lead to better results.

The impact of these meetings was immediate. The teams began to understand each other's perspectives and realized they were ultimately working toward the same organizational goals. The tension eased as communication improved and they adopted a more collaborative approach to their work. The managers' initiative to bring both teams together and build understanding turned what had been a divisive relationship into one based on cooperation, setting a new tone for how they could work together going forward.

SUPPORTING CAREER GROWTH

To build relationships strategically, it's important to recognize that career growth isn't a one-size-fits-all journey. Not everyone on your team is going to want the same thing. While some may be interested in, or dead set on, leadership roles, others might prefer to stay in an individual contributor role or even explore opportunities in different departments. As a manager, it's helpful to offer different career development options that align with each person's strengths and interests. Giving your team that flexibility is incredibly important to keep them engaged. When they see multiple ways to grow, they're more likely to stay committed and honestly share what they're interested in. If they don't want *your* job, it's better to know that now than to assume they do, prepare them for it, and then have them leave because they didn't want to hurt your feelings by telling you they wanted something else entirely.

Regular one-on-one conversations play a critical role in understanding your team members' career interests and goals. Instead of waiting for annual reviews, check in regularly and ask questions like, "What are you potentially interested in?" or "What would you like to know more about?" These open-ended questions allow employees to explore different areas without feeling confined to a single path. It's also important to ask about any skills they want to develop or challenges they're facing. By actively listening and providing tailored support, you can guide each person to figure out their career, helping them feel valued and invested in their future with the organization.

Example: A manager realized that everyone on their team assumed the only path forward was eventually to take the manager's job. This perception created unnecessary competition, and over time, some team members left, feeling there was no room for their growth. Others stayed but felt stuck. In response, the manager got leadership's buy-in to introduce multiple career development tracks, such as expert paths for those who wanted to grow their technical knowledge and leadership training for those interested in management. They held practical, candid conversations about these new opportunities and made it clear that advancement didn't have to mean taking on a management role. The shift empowered team members to consider and follow different paths, leading to higher engagement, less internal tension, and a clearer vision on how they could actually grow in the organization.

Overall, thinking strategically means that you're not just checking off today's list—you're guiding your team toward long-term success. By investing your time in their growth, you're setting the stage for them to take on more responsibilities, which frees you up to focus on higher-level priorities. Whether it's training them on new skills, mentoring them on leadership, or simply having open conversations about their goals, these investments will pay off in a stronger, more capable team.

Ultimately, strategic thinking isn't just about setting goals for the future but creating a framework where you and your team can truly work smarter, not harder. Leadership is often about making the time and space for these bigger-picture moments and then bringing your team along with you. By learning how to **Pause, Consider,** and **Act** strategically, you're equipping yourself with the tools to lead with intention, clarity, and vision.

Questions for Self-Reflection

- **How do I currently manage my time, and does it align with my long-term goals?**

  Think about whether your calendar reflects what you consider important, such as strategic planning and development, or whether it's filled with tasks that keep you in reactive mode.

- **Am I giving my team enough autonomy, or do I micromanage them?**

  Reflect on how often you check in with your team and whether you're empowering them to take ownership of their work or are staying too involved in the details.

- **What are my team's long-term goals, and how can I better align their work with the organization's objectives?**

  Consider whether you're focusing enough on how your team's contributions fit into the bigger picture and what adjustments you can make to help them achieve success beyond immediate tasks.

- **Have I built strong relationships with other departments, and how does that benefit my team?**

  Think about how often you collaborate with other managers, whether you've established effective communication, and how those relationships can support your team's goals.

- **What does strategic leadership mean to me, and how can it show up in my role?**

  Consider what steps you can take to become more strategic in your approach and help guide your team toward long-term success.

CONCLUSION

Putting It All into Practice

As a manager, you're going to face challenges every single day. Some of these challenges will seem familiar, and others will catch you off guard. When you first picked up this book, how were you feeling? Maybe you were nervous, unsure of how to handle all the responsibilities on your plate. Or maybe you were searching for guidance about how to become a better leader. Whatever it was, I hope you're now feeling more confident and excited about leadership. You have the potential to do more than just get the work done—you have the power to influence careers and make a meaningful impact on people's lives. That's what this journey is all about: taking the tools and insights you've learned and using them to create lasting change.

The message of this book is simple: You have options. With those options, you can transform the lives and careers of your team while advancing your own career and enhancing your life. That's why the **Pause-Consider-Act** framework was created—to provide you with a simple but powerful way to handle any situation that comes your way.

First, you'll pause—this isn't about stopping, but giving yourself a moment to breathe and avoid reacting on impulse. From there, you'll take a step back and consider the situation from different angles, especially from the perspective of those involved. What could the outcomes be? How might others be feeling? Instead of just thinking from your own perspective, you'll expand your thinking to include others' experiences and the potential impact on them. Then, you'll act with clarity, empathy, and confidence. This approach not only helps you make better decisions and avoid regretful reactions but also strengthens your relationships with your team. It's about leading with intention, even during the toughest moments.

The strategies and tips I've shared throughout this book don't require a huge investment of time or effort, but they can make a big impact. I've seen this firsthand, from restaurant managers handling busy shifts to senior leaders at global consulting firms navigating high-stakes decisions. None of these individuals had to change who they were to become great leaders. Instead, by making small, intentional adjustments, they became the kind of manager their employees remember as "the best they ever had." And the same can happen for you. By implementing these steps, your team can become more engaged, motivated, and productive. In turn, not only does the work get done—it gets done better because you've grown as a leader.

The goal of this book is to arm you with the tools to navigate the real challenges of management—whether it's having tough conversations, motivating your team, or holding them accountable in a way that builds trust, not fear. I want you to finish it feeling not just ready, but empowered, knowing you have what it takes to lead with confidence. And the best part? You don't have to do it alone. The exercises, examples, and actionable tools in this book are here for you to revisit anytime you need them. Imagine a team that's firing on all cylinders, where every person feels valued and motivated. And you, as their manager, standing proud, knowing you've created that environment. That's not just a dream—it's entirely possible. With the right mindset and these tools, you can create a work culture where everyone thrives—and so do you.

***

The next step in your leadership journey isn't about starting over—it's about building on everything you've already learned. These tools are here to help you deepen your impact, approach challenges with fresh insight, and lead with intention. Even as an experienced leader, there's always more to uncover, including new ways to connect with your team, sharpen your strategy, and create meaningful change that lasts.

Remember how we started this book—comparing leadership to trying to juggle walking four dogs at once? That chaotic energy felt all too real because, for so many of us, that's exactly what leading a team can feel like. But now, with the tools, prompts, and mindset you've picked up throughout these pages, that same walk feels different. There's a rhythm. You know when to pause, when to steer, and how to guide your team with clarity and care. It's not about perfect control—it's about leading with purpose, confidence, and heart.

You're not at the end—you're just finding your stride. This chapter doesn't close the book; it gives you the push to write what's next.

RESOURCES

Continue the Learning

As you've seen throughout this book, being a successful manager is an ongoing process—one that requires continued learning, reflection, and access to the right tools. To help you take these lessons even further, we've created a range of resources to support your growth and the success of your team.

If you're looking to take your leadership skills to the next level, our Manager 101 course is for you. It includes engaging videos and a comprehensive resource guide, all designed to equip you with real, actionable strategies and solutions to tackle the everyday challenges every manager faces. From leading your team with confidence to handling tough conversations, setting clear expectations, and driving results, this course equips you with practical tools you can start using right away.

If your organization is ready to strengthen its leadership from the inside out, our training packages make it simple to get started—and for the impacts to last. We don't just offer content; we give managers the tools, strategies, and support they need to lead with confidence and drive results that align with their goals. Whether you're launching Manager 101 or building on advanced leadership skills, our programs are designed for real-world impact. Each package includes everything you need to run successful internal cohorts—customized toolkits, session guides, and communications templates—so managers are equipped not just to learn, but to lead with purpose.

Whether you're looking for individual learning, team training, or a scalable program for your organization, we have a practical solution that fits your needs and sets you up for lasting success.

Learn more and access all the resources here:
managermethod.com/book

ENDNOTES

INTRODUCTION

1. Tera Allas and Bill Schaninger, "The Boss Factor: Making the World a Better Place Through Workplace Relationships," *McKinsey Quarterly*, September 22, 2020, https://www.mckinsey.com/capabilities/people-and-organizational-performance/our-insights/the-boss-factor-making-the-world-a-better-place-through-workplace-relationships.

2. "What Is Employee Engagement, and How Do You Improve It?," Gallup, April 23, 2025, https://www.gallup.com/workplace/285674/improve-employee-engagement-workplace.aspx.

CHAPTER 1

1. T. Eckert, "Managers Impact Our Mental Health More Than Doctors, Therapists—and Same as Spouses," UKG, January 24, 2023, https://www.ukg.com/about-us/newsroom/managers-impact-our-mental-health-more-doctors-therapists-and-same-spouses.

2. Marwa Azab, "The History of Imposter Syndrome," *Psychology Today*, August 22, 2023, https://www.psychologytoday.com/us/blog/neuroscience-in-everyday-life/202308/the-history-of-imposter-syndrome.

CHAPTER 3

1. Bert Gambini, "Study Shows 'Walking a Mile in Their Shoes' May Be Hazardous to Your Health," *University of Buffalo News*, May 11, 2017, https://www.buffalo.edu/news/releases/2017/05/016.html.

CHAPTER 4

1. Kimberly Gilsdorf, Fay Hanleybrown, and Dashell Laryea, "How to Improve the Engagement and Retention of Young Hourly Workers," *Harvard Business Review*, December 12, 2017, https://hbr.org/2017/12/how-to-improve-the-engagement-and-retention-of-young-hourly-workers.

2. Rachel Yi, "Employee Retention Depends on Getting Recognition Right," *Gallup Workplace*, March 13, 2023, https://www.gallup.com/workplace/650174/employee-retention-depends-getting-recognition-right.aspx.

3. "The New Performance Equation in the Age of AI," Microsoft Work Lab, April 20, 2023, http://microsoft.com/en-us/worklab/work-trend-index/the-new-performance-equation-in-the-age-of-ai.

CHAPTER 6

1. Jim Harter, "Manager Burnout Is Only Getting Worse," Gallup, December 18, 2023, https://www.gallup.com/workplace/357404/manager-burnout-getting-worse.aspx.

CHAPTER 8

1. Rebecca Zucker, "How Taking a Vacation Improves Your Well-Being," *Harvard Business Review*, July 19, 2023, hbr.org/2023/07/how-taking-a-vacation-improves-your-well-being.

2. Bill Bradley, "Lin-Manuel Miranda Says It's No Accident 'Hamilton' Inspiration Struck on Vacation," *HuffPost*, June 23, 2016, https://www.huffpost.com/entry/lin-manuel-miranda-says-its-no-accident-hamilton-inspiration-struck-on-vacation_n_576c136ee4b0b489bb0ca7c2.

3. M. Hainey, "Lin-Manuel Miranda Thinks the Key to Parenting Is a Little Less Parenting," *GQ*, April 26, 2016, https://www.gq.com/story/unexpected-lin-manuel-miranda.

4. Sarah Green Carmichael, "The Research Is Clear: Long Hours Backfire for People and for Companies," *Harvard Business Review*, August 19, 2015, https://hbr.org/2015/08/the-research-is-clear-long-hours-backfire-for-people-and-for-companies.

CHAPTER 9

1. "Enforcement and Litigation Statistics," U.S. Equal Employment Opportunity Commission, January 17, 2025, https://www.eeoc.gov/data/enforcement-and-litigation-statistics-0#tableau-viz-2.

2. "Jelly Roll's Acceptance Speech at the 2020 Country Music Awards," YouTube, November 11, 2020, https://www.youtube.com/watch?v=WTJClSQm45M.

INDEX

travel, providing information
about, 55
trust
building, 22
delegating and, 85–86
empathy and, 33
hiring process and, 42, 56
work-life balance and trusting
team members, 115–116, 127
in yourself, 13

U

UKG, 3
University of Buffalo, 31

V

vacation, need for. *See* work-life
balance

W

work-life balance, 109–135. *See also*
individuality and individual
needs
accountability for, 104–105
burnout and, 113–116
checking in without micromanaging, 120–121

checklist for, 131–133
difficulty of taking time off,
110–113
"How We Can Actually Be 'Off'
During Time Off" sessions,
123, 125–126
interviewing and providing
information about, 55
leading by example for, 133–134
new hires and interview discussions about, xviii–xx, xxii,
39–40, 41–42
during off-hours, 128–130
Pause-Consider-Act framework
for, 116–120
providing coverage for others
and respecting roles, 126–127
self-reflection questions for, 135
stress reduction with, 109–110
team members and individual
needs, 124–126
team members' time off for,
121–124
time zone differences and,
130–131
workload balance, accountability
for, 101–102, 106
worry. *See* self-doubt

Y

you've got this. *See* readiness for
leadership

ACKNOWLEDGMENTS

This book wouldn't exist without the incredible people who've shaped my life, work, and perspective on leadership.

Thank you to the entire Hay House team for your support and belief in this project, especially Cheryl Segura for making it a reality, and Sally Mason-Swaab, Karen Levy, and Lisa Bernier for your thoughtful edits and guidance throughout the process.

To the leaders, mentors, and colleagues I've been fortunate to work alongside—you taught me how to lead well and still live life outside of work.

To those who encouraged me to share these ideas more broadly—thank you for believing in this work. I'm especially grateful to the HR leaders who've brought my training into your organizations; you've made these conversations real, not just theoretical. Thank you to Alison Hankey for introducing me to LinkedIn Learning and to my *HR Besties* podcast co-hosts, Leigh Elena Henderson and Jamie Jackson, for the laughs and honest conversations along the way.

To my family—thank you for your love, support, and the constant reminder of what matters most. To my parents, Nancy and Jack, for their encouragement from day one. To my brother and in-laws, for showing up in every way that counts. To my husband, Dan, who didn't just support this work but also took the leap to join me in building Manager Method—there's no one else I'd rather be building it with. To our kids, for being my greatest motivation (and listening to me tie every life experience back to people management), and to Rosie, my constant office companion.

This book is for the managers who want to do better, for the teams counting on them, and for anyone who believes work can be human—and still get results.

ABOUT THE AUTHOR

Ashley Herd believes that when managers have clear, practical tools—and permission to be human—they can drive real results and create better workplaces for everyone. That belief comes from years of seeing all sides of leadership: from an employee on the front lines at Subway and Kmart, through her time as a legal and HR leader at global organizations, including McKinsey & Company and Yum! Brands.

As the founder of Manager Method, Ashley helps leaders build confidence and take action with practical training, ready-to-use resources, and leadership development that actually sticks. She's a LinkedIn Learning instructor and co-host of the *HR Besties* podcast, and she's known on social media (@managermethod) for bringing humor, relatability, and clear next steps to the conversations managers face every day.

Ashley lives in Atlanta with her husband, Dan, their two children, and dog (and writing companion), Rosie.

We hope you enjoyed this Hay House book. If you'd like to receive our online catalog featuring additional information on Hay House books and products, or if you'd like to find out more about the Hay Foundation, please contact:

BUSINESS

Hay House LLC, P.O. Box 5100, Carlsbad, CA 92018-5100
(760) 431-7695 or (800) 654-5126
www.hayhouse.com® • www.hayfoundation.org

———

Published in Australia by:
Hay House Australia Publishing Pty Ltd
18/36 Ralph St., Alexandria NSW 2015
Phone: +61 (02) 9669 4299
www.hayhouse.com.au

Published in the United Kingdom by:
Hay House UK Ltd
1st Floor, Crawford Corner,
91–93 Baker Street, London W1U 6QQ
Phone: +44 (0)20 3927 7290
www.hayhouse.co.uk

Published in India by:
Hay House Publishers (India) Pvt Ltd
Muskaan Complex, Plot No. 3,
B-2, Vasant Kunj, New Delhi 110 070
Phone: +91 11 41761620
www.hayhouse.co.in

———

Let Your Soul Grow

Experience life-changing transformation—one video
at a time—with guidance from the world's leading experts.

www.healyourlifeplus.com

This is an advertisement.

Write Your Book.
Grow Your Business.

AUTHORPRENEUR
MEMBERSHIP BY HAY HOUSE

Discover one of the best ways to **establish** your expertise, strategically **increase** your revenue, organically **attract** more customers, and **deliver** your message on a wider scale.

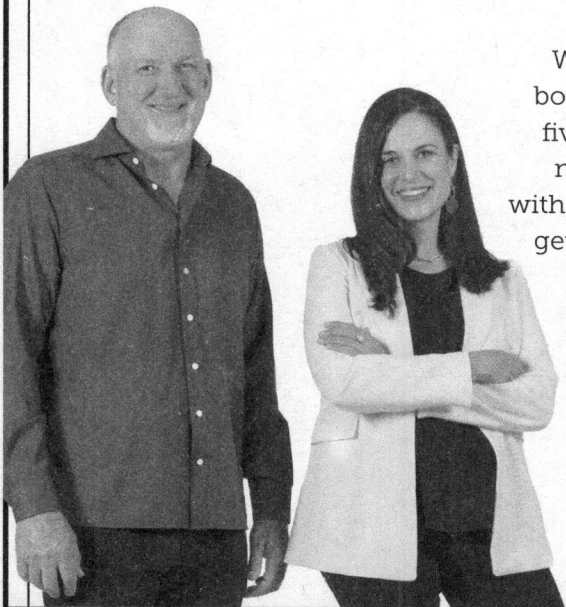

Wherever you are on the book-writing journey, our five-pathway process will meet you there. We walk with you step-by-step, from getting the book written—choosing your ideal reader, picking the best topic, outlining your material, and even finding professionals to help you—all the way through to publishing, launching, and keeping sales going.

JOIN HERE: WWW.HAYHOUSE.COM/APMEMBERSHIP

Let us show you how a book can help you reach your goals—no matter what type of business you're growing!

HAY HOUSE